NO
COMMON
SENSE

JOHN B MCMILLAN

SWEETSPIRE LITERATURE
—— MANAGEMENT ——

CONTENTS

Chapter 1: Typhoon. 1

Chapter 2: South East Asia 8

Chapter 3: White Knuckle Ride 15

Chapter 4: Champagne On The Seabed 22

Chapter 5: Watch Those Bubbles! 27

Chapter 6: Que Sera Sera 32

Chapter 7: Sometimes 36

Chapter 8: Tide Of Fortune 42

Chapter 9: Welcome To Jakarta. 48

Chapter 10: What Earthquake?. 53

Chapter 11: Eruption 59

Chapter 12: Bali 66

Chapter 13: A Trawangan Legend 70

Chapter 14: Komodo Dragons. 78

Chapter 15: Diving in That? 84

Chapter 16: Barefoot In Bat Shit. 90

Chapter 17: Deceptions. 97

Chapter 18: After The Tsunami 106

Chapter 19: On Top Of The World 111

Chapter 20: Bloodsuckers 117

Chapter 21: Sipadan 124

Chapter 22: Speaking Pidgin 134

Chapter 23: Earthquakes Galore. 141

Chapter 24: Thailand 145

Chapter 25: Birthday Mantas 156

Chapter 26: Living The Dream. 162

Chapter 27: In Bed With Two Nurses. 167

Chapter 28: A Real Man. 177

Chapter 29: Maldives 183

Chapter 30: Palau 190

Chapter 31: Yap. 195

Chapter 32: Truk Lagoon 199

Chapter 33: New Age – Old Age 205

Chapter 34: Fellowship 211

Chapter 35: A New Career 219

Chapter 36: Paralysed 223

Chapter 37: Festina Lente. 229

Chapter 38: On The Mend 234

Chapter 1

TYPHOON

In a telephone conversation with my younger son, Euan, my former colleague, Norman Kirkpatrick, said, "I have the greatest respect for your father, both as a friend and former colleague. He is an extremely intelligent man capable of a level of thought that I could never aspire to…(but when Norman makes one of those pregnant pauses after such a build-up, you know he is going to deliver the knockout punch!)…but he has absolutely no common sense!" Euan agreed. Maybe they are right. Judge for yourself.

After an overnight stop in Manila, I planned on diving at Puerto Galera, Mindoro. To get there from Manila takes a journey of about 5 hours by bus and ferry. I hailed a taxi at the hotel to take me to the bus station to catch the bus to the port of Batangas. A few moments into the journey, the driver asked me where I was planning on going, then told me, "You won't get there today. I've just heard on the radio that a typhoon warning has been issued. Should I take you back to your hotel?"

Well, if the world can play dirty tricks on you, this is one of the most likely places on earth for it to happen – or was it just bluffing? I had heard of typhoon warnings that came to nothing, just some heavy rain and a breeze. Maybe this would be the same. The track of a typhoon (known as a hurricane in the Atlantic, or a cyclone in the South Pacific and Indian Oceans) is difficult to predict. A warning is a statement of risk, not a cast-iron certainty. Ever the eternal optimist, I said, "Och, just keep going. It may come to nothing."

"I don't think so. They said it was expected to be a category five typhoon. That's a big one, the most severe."

"Och, we get hurricane force winds regularly in the north of Scotland. We call it a 'bit of a breeze' where I live."

Truth is, I like a good storm. My late wife once told me on seeing my excitement when hurricane force winds had been forecast, "You're mad. Look at you! You are never happier than when a deep depression is approaching. You can't wait to get out in it." It is always a great feeling to encounter nature at her roughest, to take appropriate action, and survive. I had that feeling of eager anticipation again.

As the bus left the city and the wide horizons of south Luzon opened up, it was clear that a classic storm was imminent. The sky had that pearl-grey look about it. The sun was a ghostly glow behind a thin sheet of high cloud, while low on the horizon storm clouds were gathering, a leaden-grey wall that promised rain, lots of rain, and behind that would come the wind. A category five typhoon, or super typhoon, has sustained wind speeds of more than 138 miles per hour (222 km/h). Comparing that with 'gale force' winds of 40 mph (64km/h) gives you an idea of what to expect. Such winds cause a lot of damage, build up enormous seas, and the accompanying rains cause extensive flooding. I felt a sense of foreboding, coupled with a build-up of excitement.

At the port of Batangas, all sailings had been cancelled. Crowds of people milled around; some looking worried, some confused, and the Filipinos among them sat around with that vacant look that said '*Que sera, sera, whatever will be, will be.*' It's as good an attitude as any in such a situation.

I reckoned hotel rooms might be difficult to find in Batangas on such a day, but I thought I might turn this to some advantage. About 30 km along the coast was Anilao, a place reputed to have good diving. With a typhoon imminent, there would be no prospect of any diving, but I could at least check the place out and maybe come back sometime. I hired a motorcycle trike to get me there. The village was tiny, with no hotels, but I found a room at a small coastal resort nearby. I was the only customer.

My room was at the end of a row, adjacent to the beach, but tucked in behind a massive sea wall. The building was of concrete block construction. Its thatch roof was netted. The windows had heavy tarpaulin covers drawn over them. I thought they might tear in a strong wind, and I was proved right, but otherwise it seemed capable of weathering a storm.

The annoying thing was that during this time there was no wind and the sea showed no more than a slight motion. Boats could easily have made the 75-minute trip across, but I know how quickly things can change at sea. I had no choice but to sit tight, wait, and ride out the storm when it came. I strolled down to the village to see what Anilao looked like. There wasn't much to see. A few fisherman's huts along the shore, a string of dive resorts further round the bay, and a main street with a few shops all selling the same things: food, clothing, phone cards, cooked food (but when was it cooked?), and that was it. Everything was closed by 6 p.m. There was no nightlife here. Which was just as well, as by that time the storm was beginning to make its presence felt.

With nothing else to do, I was in bed by 7 p.m. reading a book. I gave that up at 8:30 p.m. when I was plunged into darkness. The electricity power lines had fallen casualty to the force of the wind and fallen trees. I shut my eyes to the howling, banging, and crashing that was going on outside, as wind and waves thrashed the coast in fury, and slept through all this until 1:30 a.m. The shrieking of the wind then had an intensity that forced all desire for sleep out of the mind. This was something to *live* through. At least, I hoped I would live through it. All we need now, I thought, is an earthquake to create a tsunami, to coincide with the typhoon, and then I would be having a vintage Philippines experience! Two or three for the price of one is not uncommon here. I had that peculiar mixture of fear, fascination, and elation that I always get in a fierce storm, and an overpowering desire to be part of it. I grabbed my torch and got out of bed. I was standing in water. A tide of rain-water was being forced under the door. And more was dribbling in through the roof. I opened the door and shone my torch out.

Enormous frothing waves rose out of the gloom and thumped the sea wall, sending shudders right through the walls of my room. Spray flew skywards, mingled, and fell with the torrential rain that had saturated the thatched roof. Coconuts were hurtling through the air like cannon balls, thumping into walls and roofs. Branches, ripped off trees, flew like spears through the darkness. The ground was deep in debris: leaves, driftwood, nuts, branches, and water several inches deep.

If you had a desire to get yourself killed, this was the night to fulfil it. I pondered on the probability that I could walk from my hut to the gate and remain alive. It would be similar to walking into a hail of machine-gun fire, a life expectancy measured in seconds, with so much stuff flying through the air with lethal force. Several trees were down. I decided to keep my interest theoretical. This was not a night to be out in at all.

Curiosity satisfied, I went back to bed, but not before I had taken some additional precautions. I reckoned this must now be about the height of the typhoon's ferocity. I packed my rucksack, sat it on the bed to keep it out of the rising tide of water that surged under the door, and had everything ready for a quick getaway, just in case. If that were to happen, the odds of survival were not in my favour, but at least I felt I was keeping my options open. It feels better to have done something. Like putting on a lifejacket when an aircraft is about to plunge into the sea, it is unlikely to save your life, but it will make it easier for search parties to find your body. I climbed into bed again and closed my eyes.

A few minutes later, I heard the rising wail of the wind. The building began to shudder. I could feel the air pressure build up in my ears. Heavy, hard things were attacking my walls and roof. How much more can it take? I wondered. Like an approaching high-speed train with its whistle blowing, the wind rose in a fearful, screaming crescendo. Lying flat on my back, every muscle tensed. I trembled, sweated with anticipation, excitement – and fear!

With a crack like a gunshot, I sat bolt upright. As I did so, I heard the tinkling sound of broken glass crashing down behind me on the bed. The curtain rail above the window ripped itself off the wall, and with the curtain still attached, flew around in the vortex of air that spun around my room as the wind howled through the broken window, before draping itself over me. Was this to be my shroud?

Looking on the bright side (why am I optimistic in the worst of conditions, yet can be miserable with minor mishaps?) I thought, well, at least the broken window helps to compensate for the failure of the electricity supply, which had rendered my ceiling fan inoperable. The wind had taken over as its power supply and I now had plenty of air circulating. But where was the broken glass? I shone my torch and there, sticking into the recess in the pillow where my head had lain, was an arrowhead of glass about 18 inches long. That would have skewered me in the eye, digging deep thorough the eye-socket into the brain and killing me, had I not reacted so quickly to the crack of the breaking glass.

I smiled with satisfaction. My speed of reaction had not diminished with age. That must have been the quickest sit-up I ever performed. It's comforting to know you can still do it when you have to. I felt the odds of survival were improving.

The situation called for some re-assessment. The leak in the roof was worse and water was pouring on to the bed. I slid the bed to the opposite side of the room. This also reduced the risk of injury should any more glass decide to share a pillow with me. I repositioned my rucksack on the bed, between me and the hole that was once a window. That offered further defence against glass and other flying objects, for who knows what else might come zooming in through the hole. Having satisfied myself that all possible precautions had been taken and that luck was on my side, I fell asleep. I was unaware of anything else until 6:30 a.m.

One of the staff of the resort came down to check that I was still alive, and seemed relieved to find me so, and in good spirits despite the events of the night. I had repositioned the bed and the arrowhead of glass so that she could see how near I had been to death, or disfigurement. The poor girl was horrified at the thought of finding me lying there in a pool of blood with a glass arrow sticking out of my eye socket. She moved me to a room at the opposite end of the row, as far from the sea and wind as possible. Not that it mattered then. The worst was over.

The scene in the grey light of dawn was one of utter devastation. Palms, torn and forlorn, most denuded, looked like giant matchsticks. Other trees bore scars where branches had been ripped from them; some still clinging like broken limbs, dangling in the breeze. Fallen trees, broken branches, twigs, leaves, and palm fronds obliterated footpaths and roadways. Hundreds of coconuts lay like spent cannon balls on a battlefield. It looked like a typhoon had struck the place.

I was happy to have lived through it without injury. Happy too were the frogs: so much rain had fallen and created lakes where none had existed before. And the frogs celebrated. The noise of their croaking was deafening, like a crowd at a football match. I have never heard anything like it. It put a smile on my face. There is always something to be cheery about.

Typhoon 'Durian' had indeed been a category five storm. In the Philippines, the number of fatalities was in the thousands with hundreds more reported missing. In the Bicol province a huge landslide of volcanic ash, turned to slurry by the rains, had swept down the hillside and swallowed up entire villages, and the people in them. Many have never been found.

The following day, I managed to get a boat over to Sabang Beach on the Puerto Galera peninsula. The village resembled the aftermath of an air raid. Roofless buildings stood forlorn, smoke curled upwards from fires burning the wreckage of homes and fallen branches, and from all over the bay came the sound of hammering as men repaired damaged buildings. The electricity supply had still not been restored when I left after more than two weeks there, but hotels and restaurants had their own generators. Without power to operate the pumps that sucked water from the ground wells, many homes and guest houses had no water supply. Young men pushed large barrows filled with water bottles and gas cylinders to supply homes and restaurants. The local telecommunications mast was a useless stump, having had its top blown away. Cash machines at the banks and card readers in the shops could not operate.

The trees looked like they had been sprayed with weed-killer: defoliated, with drooping, broken branches. Their pitiful state had changed the landscape. Clearings had been created and houses that had previously been hidden were now exposed, many with windows and doors blown in, or with roofs missing. Yet, as in the bombed cities of Europe in the Second World War, the people were resilient. Life went on as usual and, apart from the power loss and water supply problems, it was easy to forget after only a few days that it had ever happened.

Another typhoon struck ten days later. The greying skies had all the tell-tale signs. The sea, smooth as silk, flexed its muscle in a restless swell, its thump and hiss on the shore an ominous warning of what was to come. The air was still and silent. Nature held her breath before another onslaught. The rain arrived that night, and then came the wind.

This time we were lucky: the centre of the storm had tracked well to the south of us. But Boracay, the major tourist island in the Philippines, had not been so fortunate: hundreds of trees were blown down, several resorts trashed, boats were sunk, and at least a hundred people were missing.

We had torrential rain. The one road that leads into the village down a steep hill became a river, knee deep in muddy brown water. My roof had leaked and I had another puddle on the floor, but I slept well.

And well away from the window!

Chapter 2
SOUTH EAST ASIA

My yearning to visit the islands of the South Pacific had been nourished by my reading when I was young. Attractive images had formed in my mind and were reinforced by my travels, as described in my previous books, *Recapturing Youth* and *Around The World in a Kilt*, but being largely ignorant of Thailand, Vietnam, Cambodia, Malaysia, Myanmar (formerly Burma), the Philippines, and Indonesia, I had never felt the same desire to visit the countries of South-East Asia. What knowledge I had was more of a negative nature, gleaned from reading about World War II, when the allied forces encountered not only a formidable enemy, but tropical diseases that claimed many lives: malaria, beri-beri, typhoid, dysentery, and dengue fever. That didn't sound too cheery.

In the post-war years the British army had been engaged in anti-terrorist activities in Malaysia. In the 1960s and 1970s, the US forces had become involved in, and disentangled themselves from the Vietnam War. Millions lost their lives under the oppressive Pol Pot regime in Cambodia. Political instability and corruption emerged in the Philippines and Indonesia, as well as outbursts of terrorist activity and kidnappings by separatist groups. That didn't sound very cheery either.

The South Pacific islanders had not been averse to practicing cannibalism, but that died out in the 19th century. However, in some of the remote mountain valleys in Sumatra, Papua, and Borneo, it has been reported within the last few decades that headhunters still practice their art. In such places 'having you over for dinner' could mean you might be on the menu! That fate befell an over-zealous missionary who, ignoring all advice, ventured into the interior of Papua to 'save' a tribe of cannibals – and helped to do just that by ensuring they did not starve. They ate not only him, but his wife and children as well.

South-East Asia seemed an uneasy sort of place, but how wrong that impression proved to be. Having listened to some travellers who had visited these countries, heard about the welcoming people, delicious food, stunning scenery, and superb diving, I had to find out for myself.

I enjoy independent travel, but my experience of trekking in a guided group in the Patagonian mountains had proved that it was a good way to gain some initial experience of a country where the language and transport may present some difficulties. Having a local guide who knows the language and can organise the transport arrangements is a big advantage until you develop enough confidence in your ability to communicate and manage by yourself.

I had no qualms about going to the Philippines as English is one of the official languages there, but for my first visits to Indonesia, Borneo, Thailand, and Vietnam I joined organised adventure tours. They offered an introduction to the way of life of the indigenous people and their culture, and provided opportunities for exploration. I had no hesitation in returning as an independent traveller to these places after that.

Crossing a street in any city in South East Asia seems impossible, but you only need the kind of faith that enabled Jesus to walk on water. Casting all vestiges of common sense aside, you boldly go where no sane person would dream of going, and step forward into the flow of traffic. Tourists gasp in horror. But if you show the anarchic drivers that you are as crazy and anarchic as they are, you earn their respect, and they dodge around you as you cleave a path through the mass of steel that surges along the road. And your faith in miracles is restored.

Manila traffic

I had hired a motorbike to get around in the Cook Islands. But here? No way! Well, that was how I felt at first, but after coming to the Philippines a few times and settling in one location for three months, I became as crazy as the rest of them. On the roads you have to be a committed anarchist or you'll go nowhere. You need the 'I'm not stopping for anyone or anything' attitude. My taxi driver once drove straight through a red light at a pedestrian crossing with people walking across it.

"Don't you ever stop when there is a red light and people crossing?"

"There was enough space between them for me to drive through."

In Indonesia, queuing is an alien concept. At airports they walk up to the desk and try to barge in beside the person who is being checked in, hordes of them, whole families with their bags and string-tied cardboard boxes (they always travel with cardboard boxes), with no respect for privacy or orderliness. The line painted on the floor that tells you to Wait Here, is treated like the traffic lights. It is of no consequence. You have to become an anarchist at the airport too, and use your luggage to defend your place against usurpers, shunting them out of the way as they try to jump the queue. It is a delightfully de-civilising experience.

Shopping? Labels with prices on them are meaningless. Everything is available at a price, but only the one on the price tag if you are naïve. Haggle. If you keep shaking your head they will often ask for *your* price. If they accept that immediately, even though it may be half the quoted price, then you know you've been ripped off.

Thailand is a popular place for silly European tourists to fry themselves on the beaches. You can almost smell the flesh roasting. It's hard to believe after all the warnings about sunburn and skin cancer, but there they lie, turning lobster-pink on sun-baked beaches. It is painful even to watch. They become ugly, blister, skin peels off them, and they can become very sick, unable to sleep, vomiting even, as the radiation from the sun has given them a dose of what it is like to survive a nuclear bomb. These are the people who tell you they don't want nuclear power because of their fear of radiation, yet they pay lots of money to risk a good dose of skin cancer by lying in the blistering sun.

Bali is a popular destination for Australian tourists. At least they have some respect for the sun and paint their faces grotesquely white with sun block, to the extent that they look like Hollywood versions of naked savages. Just as hordes of noisy British holiday-makers plague the Mediterranean coastal resorts, Bali becomes infested by many of the less attractive kind of Australians. Often over-sized (you never see a small Aussie), loud-mouthed, (is there such a thing as a quiet Aussie?), they waddle along the street in sagging sleeveless vests exposing armpits that are hairier than a wombat's belly, a cigarette in one hand, and a beer bottle in the other – and the men look even worse!

Thailand and the Philippines are popular with chemically dependent older men, often escorted by beautiful young ladies, at a price. They are prey for the street touts selling condoms and Viagra. And if you don't have an attractive escort, the assumption seems to be that you are there to find one.

"Viagra sir? I give you good price."

"I don't need Viagra!"

"Oh, you no have lady?"

You can see the pity in their eyes. But these guys are entrepreneurs, they see an opportunity.

"I get you sexy lady, very cheap. Take to your hotel, no problem. Stay with you all night. Give you good service. I fix it for you."

Not only does he offer to set you up for the night, he offers you the fuel to make it last all night long, a double deal! "You buy Viagra, sir, give you powah (power). I give you discount, very good price. Good for you, good for me!" He smiled and winked.

I smiled and winked back. "No thank you. I don't want sexy lady."

"Oh, you prefer lady-boy? No problem, I can fix you up." They never give up. Oh, by the way, I did not want a lady-boy either!

There are fixers everywhere. They wait at the airport arrivals hall looking for the tourist with a lost look. "Taxi, sir? This way." They call the driver up on a mobile phone. What they don't tell you is that it will cost you at least twice what you would pay if you walked outside to the taxi rank.

It can be very cheap to eat in South East Asia, and the choice of food is amazing. But beware of those fiery Thai chilli's! I always ask when ordering, "Is this very spicy?" If the waitress says, "A little bit spicy," forget it. Swallow some sulphuric acid instead. It will be kinder to your stomach. Those little red Thai chillis are devastating. They strip your tongue and lips of skin and burn out your innards. They go tearing through your digestive system like hot coals, all night long, and when you feel them burning their way out of your rear end in the morning, don't expect relief, for they'll burn you there just as bad as they did when they went in. The Thais love them and heap them into the food. I always pick out the red bits. There are vicious green ones too. Most of the food is very good and full of flavour, but I baulked at the prospect of eating Balut, a Filipino delicacy. It is an egg, boiled just before the chicken is about to emerge, so when you crack it open you are confronted by a cooked baby, eyes and beak and toes all formed. I couldn't bring myself to eat that, but they claim it adds to your vitality. "Good for old man. Gives you powah," they tell you.

One bit of advice I offer travellers at new year is to find a quiet place to stay during the celebrations. This is a time for family reunions and parties, and the essential element in any good Filipino party is a karaoke machine! Usually rented for the day, the Filipinos cannot resist them and murder all the popular songs. They all sing the same songs, but not at the same time, and in all the wrong keys. It is extreme noise pollution. Add to that a cacophony of sound from car horns, revving up motor cycle engines, the screech of hand-held horns, firecrackers, even guns. Anything that makes a noise is an essential requirement for New Years Eve celebrations.

A stroll around town at 7 p.m on New Years Eve hinted at what was to come. The streets were already thronging with people. A band was playing at full volume – that is how they measure of the quality of the music! The local fire brigade was laying out hoses along the street in anticipation. A strong police presence, supported by an armed military force with assault rifles at the ready, hinted that there might be some high spirits. This was the kind of night to stay at home.

That new year in Manila, more than 400 people were hurt or killed by powerful firecrackers in the New Year's Eve celebrations, including a 7 year-old girl who was fighting for her life after being hit on the head by a stray bullet, fired by an unidentified person at the height of the revelry. At least eight people were hit by what was described as 'celebratory gunfire!' One man had his hand blown off while lighting a prohibited firecracker labelled 'Goodbye Philippines.' But it was goodbye to his hand.

These incidents came despite the arrests of more than 300 vendors and users of illegal large fireworks in the Philippines ahead of New Year's Eve. The crackdown however was de-valued by an incident in which several policemen were seen on video helping themselves to boxes of confiscated firecrackers shortly after they were shown to reporters at a news conference. That's the Philippines for you!

Thailand is also fireworks crazy. Idiots acquire things the size of artillery shells and set them off in streets crowded with people. One went off with an enormous bang a few metres from me and was followed a few seconds later by the clang of a steel shell case landing on the street. It could have killed someone. A few minutes later one did. We came across a crowd of people around a man lying on the street. He had tried to set off a similar firework, but it failed to ignite. He went back to ignite it again, but as he bent over it, it went off and killed him. That showed more than a lack of common sense. It was madness.

Getting to South-East Asia is relatively easy with flights from the UK and the rest of Europe to the major hubs: Hong Kong, Bangkok, Kuala Lumpur, Singapore, from where you can connect to almost anywhere else. Several budget airlines offer good prices on both domestic and international routes. In Indonesia, published schedules, time keeping, standards of comfort, and reliability of aircraft are variable, and when you see the flight attendants crossing themselves and praying before take-off, you know you have signed up for an adventure!

Travelling around South East Asia is not difficult, although some journeys can be a bit of an adventure. Ferries to the islands? They have a habit of sinking in the Philippines. Sometimes it is the only way, but don't expect the standards you would expect of shipping in Europe or North America. Flights are a more reliable and comfortable option where possible. Buses are cheap, but you pay to get transported, not to be comfortable. And if you decide to take a bus trip into the mountainous regions, you could be in for a thrill.

Chapter 3

WHITE KNUCKLE RIDE

Taking a break from diving, I wanted to visit Banaue to see the amazing rice terraces carved out of the Cordillera Mountains, the rocky backbone of Luzon, largest of the Philippine islands. I hadn't realised how big this island was, but after interminable hours in clapped-out buses and rickety jeepneys, both me and my aching backside now know better.

The journey began in Manila in an air-conditioned bus, comfortable by Philippine standards. Six hours later, I had exchanged the sweaty mayhem of Manila and the sultry heat of the patchwork of rice fields on the plains, for refreshing mountain breezes in the city of Baguio, at around 5,000 feet altitude. But that was only the beginning. I had a long way to go yet.

Why pay for budget-bursting, thrill-seeking, bungy-jumping and sky-diving when you can have (for only a few pesos) a nine-hour, terrifying ride in a ramshackle bus through the most catastrophe-prone country in the world with its killer typhoons, earthquakes, torrential rains, floods, and landslides – and where I was heading was the place to get them.

A recent super-typhoon and its torrential rain had resulted in floods on the plains and landslides in the mountains. The road I was on disappeared into a lake where water buffalo wallowed as though in paradise, with only their dopey, horny heads showing above water. Anyone with a grain of common sense would have turned round and gone home, but our crazy driver plunged into it without hesitation, and managed to navigate through the lake without ever straying from the submerged road. He even managed to drive round an underwater bend in the road. You have to admire these guys. They may drive like maniacs, but they do get you there in one piece – sometimes.

The road, I mean proper road, as we would recognise one in our developed countries, didn't last long after Baguio, a pleasant city with a climate like Scotland in summer: cool and wet. Even the beds had blankets and duvets on them, unlike the rest of the Philippines where you need air conditioning to maintain a reasonable temperature for sleeping. After only a few miles of road with a concrete surface, we reached the first landslide. It had swept away a section of concrete that now lay half-way down the mountain. They had filled the gap with rubble, and without a care in the world, the bus drove over it. A few miles on, we hit a dirt road. But with most of the dirt washed away by the torrential rains, it was in skeletal form – bare rock, some hard and unyielding, some loose. It was like driving along a river-bed with a steep mountain towering above, threatening to throw more of itself down upon us with every drop of rain that fell. On the other side (there was no barrier of any sort), a rocky slope led down 1000 feet to a foaming river that would be the destination of all our bits and pieces if another landslide did occur, for survival was unimaginable if we went over the edge.

One section of road was carved into a vertical rock face. The rock was almost scraping one side of the bus and offered only a few inches of headroom above the roof. On the open side, all I saw was a sheer drop down hundreds of feet. How close the bus wheels were to the edge, I could only imagine, but it was more comfortable not to. I could not even see the edge. To add to the pleasure for thrill seekers, at the end of this half-tunnel a landslide had taken away at least half the road. Undeterred, our driver swept his bus through the torrent of water that still rushed over what was left of the road, and past the water-swept gully that had once been our side of the road. And it was still being eroded by the rush of water.

Our driver showed not the slightest vestige of fear, nor hesitation in executing any manoeuvre, and there were plenty to be executed. He had a fiendish grin on his face as he hurled his bus round hairpin bends and took us to the brink of extinction on precipitous cliffs where no bus should ever have been, or so we would think in our safety-conscious world. But this was the Philippines, where life is fun despite the catastrophes and endemic poverty. Marvelling at the skill with which he took us so close to extinction, yet always brought us back just short of having cardiac arrest, it was impossible not to develop an overwhelming confidence in him; a confidence that grew almost to the point of hero-worship. And I began to enjoy the ride, revelling in the thrill of it all. The nightmares came later, as I lay in the darkness, re-playing the action in my mind.

And that was only the first six hours of the trip north from Baguio to Sagada. Another three hours of buttock-crushing, knuckle-clenching, lip-biting, heart-stopping travel by jeepney was in store to get me to Banaue after that. But that was for the next day. Why cram all the fun into one day? Spread it about a bit!

Elderly Igorot woman

Drained with all the excitement, it was a relief to explore the sleepy village of Sagada, a place noted for its cliffs and limestone caves with hanging coffins. Tradition is still strong among the Igorot people who inhabit these mountains, and it is not unusual to see men wandering along the road wearing just a G-string and loincloth. The women wear colourful head-dress. This is frontier territory.

It is reputed to be head-hunter country, and inter-tribal wars are not uncommon. The government seldom bothers to intervene in these disputes, allowing the tribes to settle their grievances in the traditional ways. They don't involve outsiders, so they don't harm anyone but themselves, but if you are trekking in these mountains it is best to have a local guide to ease things along for you. Hotels? Camp sites? Toilets? Forget all that. Trekking up here means you go native; squat in the bush, and leave a feast for the pigs, which may well accompany you in eager anticipation as you seek some privacy. There is a primitive satisfaction in reverting to nature.

More rough and tumble, slithering, and scrambling over landslides that had piled earth and rubble over the roads, engaged the imagination in all sorts of horror scenarios in the three-hour jeepney ride that took me to Banaue and what has been called the eighth wonder of the world (one of the *three* eighth wonders in the Philippines!), the astonishing rice terraces.

Banaue rice terraces

18

Think of a forty-five degree mountain slope – and that is steep – and imagine cutting a series of ledges out of it to give some flat land to grow rice and other vegetables. To support these ledges are retaining walls, some as high as ten feet, the stone work packed with clay to retain water. The rice fields require irrigation, so water has to be ducted in and out as required. Multiply this by the effort required to build thousands of such terraces along the mountainsides, following their contours for mile after mile. These were built by the small Igorot people two thousand years ago or more, with only the most basic hand tools. It is a remarkable feat of labour and presents an astonishing sight.

Banaue is a grim-looking, grey town clinging to the steep sides of the mountain. The front door of a house may be at road level, but the back of the house could be supported by stilts with a drop of 10 to 20 metres to the ground below it, so steep are the slopes upon which they are built. Here you find people living and working in a way we, in the so-called developed countries, find difficult to imagine. It is a town of rice farmers and craftsmen, wood carvers in particular. Their carvings are sometimes immense, often statues of human figures and animals, but those I liked best were the ones made from tree roots, their natural form inspiring semi-abstract creations.

Betel nut and tobacco chewing is common and the streets are sprinkled with great gobs of spittle. It looked like someone had been running around bleeding to death.

The trip back to Manila was also eventful. Is ever a trip in the Philippines not eventful, I began to wonder? The air-conditioned bus direct from Banaue was booked for two days ahead, so I travelled native again. The first leg, from Banaue down to the plains to the east, was another rough, bum-bashing mountain ride in a packed jeepney. Several passengers were sitting on the roof; others clung to the sides with not a care in the world.

Always room for one more!

Three hours later, down on the main road, I caught another bus heading towards Manila. It wasn't any more comfortable than the jeepney. Its tired seats, having supported more bums than they were ever designed for, had long ceased to offer any cushioning effect, but this is the Philippines where such things are ignored. These buses also never refuse a fare. As more passengers climbed aboard, folding seats were pulled out, offering seats in the aisle, which made it quite a performance when anyone at the back of the bus had to get off. Our over-loaded and over-worked old bus ploughed its sweaty way (no air-con, on this bus, no windows either, just open sides) back down through the rice fields in the baking sun. But the excitement wasn't over yet. In late afternoon, the engine suddenly raced out of control and threatened to shake itself off its mountings – and gave us a good shaking too – and with these death throes it expired in an impressive cloud of steam. Death due to overheating: our bus wasn't going any further.

We all piled out and flagged down other overcrowded buses, snatching seats where we could get them. My next bus was full, not just of people, but sacks of rice, vegetables, chickens, baskets, suitcases, baby-chairs, and anything else that people wanted to transport. The only available seat was at the rear of the bus, and to get there I had to scramble over these obstacles packed in the aisle, and past a tethered goat. Eleven hours after leaving Banaue, without breakfast, lunch, or dinner, I arrived back in Manila, having survived on bottled water and dried mangoes.

That's travelling in the Philippines for you.

Chapter 4

CHAMPAGNE ON THE SEABED

It's More Fun In The Philippines proclaim the tourist brochures, and to some extent that is true. As a novel way to bring in the New Year at Moalboal on Cebu Island, Savedra Dive Centre had organised a short night dive, just before mid-night on December 31st, to toast the arrival of the new year by sharing a bottle of champagne – underwater! Where else but in the Philippines would you think of drinking champagne while sitting on the seabed with 10 metres of ocean above you?

Eleven divers signed up for it. A few minutes before mid-night, we entered the water from the shore. Sitting in a circle on the sand at 10 metres depth, our torches lit up the scene as the clock ticked its way to mid-night.

When January 1 arrived, the divemaster inverted the bottle and eased out the cork. The pressure of the sea at that depth is twice the surface air pressure, and with the bottle upside down, that forces the champagne to stay inside the bottle.

You remove your regulator from your mouth, raise the bottle to your lips and blow air into it. The air rises to the top (which is the bottom of the bottle because it is now upside-down) from where it cannot escape. The air you blow in forces the champagne downwards, out of the bottle, and into your mouth. And the more air you put in, the more champagne you get out. You then pass the bottle on to the diver next to you, and it circulates around the group.

You swallow the champagne and put your breathing apparatus back in your mouth. This is important, otherwise you will breathe in seawater and spoil the taste of the champagne – not to mention the risk of death by drowning. In the resulting euphoria, it is easy to forget that you are sitting on the floor of the ocean.

By the time you shake hands with those around you to wish them a happy new year, the bottle has come round to you again and you have another swig. It is well-known that diving and alcohol do not mix well, so that was the limit and we returned to join the festivities ashore. It was an unforgettable way to start the year.

My dive buddy there was a lithe, 63 year-old woman called Annabelle who had been diving for about 40 years. Trained as a diver in the South African Navy, she had logged thousands of dives. Very efficient with her breathing, she found that I was the only other diver in the group who could come close to matching her in air consumption, so she told the dive manager that she wanted me – no one else!– as a dive buddy. It was a nice compliment. It suited me too. I wanted time to take photos, and she was happy to scout around to find interesting subjects for me.

On New Year's Day, the rest of the group paddled off and left us behind. We surfaced after 71 minutes. When I climbed aboard the boat, the divemaster smiled. "Good dive?"

"Very good. A great way to start the New Year."

The others were not smiling. A weather front with a cold wind and rain had brought a chilling drop in temperature, and they had been shivering for over 20 minutes waiting for us. I smiled at them. "Sorry to keep you waiting." I wasn't, but I felt I had to say something placatory. No one smiled back. I turned to Annabelle who was sitting with her back to them divesting herself of her dive gear.

"I don't think we are very popular, John," she muttered, "but it was a wonderful dive to start the New Year. Thank you for being my buddy."

23

Sardines. Hardly a word to get you excited, is it? Not like cries of, "Whale Shark!" or "Manta!" You can't imagine many divers hyperventilating about coming face to face with a sardine.

However, imagine you are a diver, 25 metres down on a bright, sunny day with good visibility. You are cruising along an undersea cliff festooned with soft corals. Multi-coloured butterflyfish and angelfish dart in and out of the labyrinthine tunnels that perforate the coral. The occasional lone shark patrols below you, gliding through the depths.

It darkens, as though you had entered a cave. You look up to see if you had drifted under a rock overhang, but it is not rock that stops the light getting to you.

It is sardines. Millions of them. Like a dark storm cloud, they hover above you. But how far does this huge shoal of fish extend? 100 metres? 200 metres? More? It is impossible to tell, for it extends far beyond the range of visibility.

Sardines

We approach from below. With startling rapidity the shoal of tiny fish reacts as though it were one. Millions of fish, alerted by the perceived threat of the approaching divers, dart and sway, the cloud they create forming surreal patterns in the ocean. How they all know we are getting near is a mystery as you cannot see more than a few centimetres into the school, such is the density of the fish within it. Yet the panic reaction of the fish around the periphery seems enough to alert, in a split second, every one of the millions of fish to take evasive action, all at the same time.

The shoal swings and sways, sunlight flashing from their silver sides as they turn. A diver with a camera approaches the underbelly of the cloud and it opens, creating a vertical tunnel all the way to the surface, with sunlight shafting down though the tube. The diver moves to one side to get a closer picture and it metamorphoses into a giant wave, like a tsunami about to break on a beach, its surface streaked with silver as the fish propel themselves away in terror, tiny tails working so fast it is almost impossible to discern the movement.

Any slight change in the environment causes it to surge and sway, tumbling like a breaking wave, or opening like a huge mouth about to swallow the invader. It is fascinating, awesome, almost frightening in appearance; for although each fish is so tiny, the sheer scale of the mass of bodies is overwhelming. It seems to develop a group personality and dynamic that dominates each individual within it. Like a crowd out of control, it has lost all reason, responding only in mass panic, dissipating its energies in flight.

Despite its often surreal and sometimes threatening appearance – large, black, swaying, nightmarish thing that it is – it contains no more threat than that of any one small fish within it. It is all about appearance, not substance. As the hairs on a dog or cat become erect when threatened to give a larger more menacing aspect to their appearance, so too does this enormous shoal of fish create an illusion of power.

To be down there in close proximity to it brought a new understanding of the lives of my ancestors in the 19th century; fishermen who went to sea with their nets in small open boats in pursuit of the sardine's Scottish cousin, the herring. Referred to as the silver darlings, they brought prosperity to many coastal communities. I remember being told that when a net surrounded the shoal of herring, they were so densely packed they could be scooped up in baskets.

Old fishermens' tales? No, not after seeing the density of that shoal of sardines.

The sardines had become the star attraction since arriving off Moalboal a few months earlier. But where did they come from? And why? When will they leave again? Will there be a command from the King Sardine, if there is one, unlikely as that may be, that all others will follow? How do they communicate with each other so that they can react as one and never collide with each other, always maintaining a few millimetres separation between neighbours. And when they do move on, how do they decide where to go next? It was one of the most fascinating sights I have witnessed underwater.

Having been there once before for only a few days, I was amazed at the number of people who recognised me. Panagsama Beach, where the dive shops are located, has one dirt road that masquerades as a street and everyone soon gets to know you. The shopkeepers sitting at their wee stalls speak to you as you pass, ask your name, where you are from, how long you are staying. That's what I like about small places: you get to know the people and they get to know you. But how could they remember me from among the thousands of visitors they see each year?

Dina, the lady who cleaned the rooms at the resort, chatted to me often and invited me to her grand-daughter's fourth birthday party. A whole roasted pig waited to be eaten, followed by a delicious fruit salad, with plenty to drink. But I had the only white face there: none of the other guests at the resort had been invited. Why me? Is it the Scottish accent? Or the kilt?

Other than that, I am just a quiet, nondescript individual...like a sardine.

Chapter 5

WATCH THOSE BUBBLES!

Everyone knows that if you release air underwater the bubbles float up to the surface. Right? But when you are diving and you see your bubbles descending into the depths of the ocean instead of rising upwards, it may cause a degree of disorientation. What is happening to the laws of nature? Why are your bubbles going down, to be swallowed in the depths – and you with them? You don't need a depth gauge to let you know you are going down; your ears hurt as the pressure increases.

"Watch those bubbles!" was a bit of advice in an email from Josh, my dive guide on my first trip into Burmese waters. He had written of his latest adventure at Flores, Indonesia. He was on an invitation-only expedition, exploring places where the currents were extreme and no diver had dared to venture before. It was for experienced dive professionals, the guides who operate in the turbulent waters around the myriad of islands on that volcanic chain of islands that stretches from Java to Papua.

He described one of those washing-machine dives where the current did everything to disorientate the diver, where the down current was so strong that even the air bubbles did not go floating up to the surface as they should, but were dragged into the depths and compressed, defying the laws of nature. He and his co-divers survived the ordeal and, knowing that I have a wee bit of a thirst for adventure, offered that reminder: 'If you are diving in strong turbulent currents, watch those bubbles.' A week later, his words were ringing in my ears.

We had crossed Sogod Bay, from Padre Burgos in South Leyte to Panaon Island, to dive around a headland called Napantao. At the headland, some rocks protruded above the surface. Each had a bow-wave like a ship, as the current raged past them. Beyond that, the sea erupted in a tormented dance of irregular conical waves. Whirlpools and eddies streaked with foam swirled and sucked air into the depths. I had experienced the forces at play in such waters and how they can toss a 15-ton yacht around. What might they do to a handful of divers? I expected our guide to apply some common sense and say, "No diving here today."

"This is the number one dive site in South Leyte," he said. But with a look of concern, he added, "It also has the number one current." He paused for a moment. "Okay, we go diving. Current is going this way so we go with it, keeping the wall on our left."

Well, the current was going "this way" out there in the deep water, but the headland had caused an eddy in the bay on the north side where the boat dropped us, and in there it was flowing the opposite way. We finned our way down to gather on the bottom, otherwise the current would have had scattered us before we even began. Grouping there, we then had to fight against the current towards the cliff that dropped down to the sea floor, 1500 metres (nearly 5000 feet) below.

After clawing ourselves across a slope, we reached a patch of slack water close to the cliff where we could rest for a moment. Ablaze with colour and populated with hundreds of fish, I gazed in wonder at one of the most impressive walls I have seen, but not for long. The sea wanted to play with us.

Drifting towards the headland, the current picked up again, sweeping us along with increasing velocity. I noticed the fish a few metres ahead were not horizontal. They were standing on their tales, an indication of a powerful down current, and I heard Josh's words in my ears: "Watch those bubbles!"

My bubbles, instead of soaring up to the surface, were now going downwards, compressed in size from that of an apple, to that of a golf ball, and then to the size of a marble by the increasing pressure of the deeper water despite my kicking against the downward thrust. My ears were already feeling as though six-inch nails were being pushed into them. One hand was on my inflator button, pumping more air in to compensate for the downward thrust, the other squeezing my nose as I blew into it to equalise the pressure on my ears. The ears popped, and I checked the depth reading on my dive computer. I had dropped about 15 metres in a few seconds and was still descending. I pumped more air into my buoyancy vest and felt it tighten around me. At last, my balloon-like shape now arrested the descent.

My mind was thinking ahead. Where you get strong down currents, you may also find, a few moments later, some strong upward currents – and these are more dangerous. With my buoyancy vest filled with air in an upward current, that would accelerate me in a rapid ascent, a life-threatening situation. The volume of air in your lungs doubles every 10 metres you ascend, threatening to rupture your lungs if you do not get it out quickly enough. Micro bubbles of nitrogen can form in your blood stream and that can lead to decompression sickness, 'The Bends,' which can lead to paralysis, or death. Having stopped myself plummeting to the ocean floor thousands of feet below, I was anticipating what might happen next – and it did!

Without any warning it felt like a big hand was lifting me upwards as fast as the bubbles, not a good sign at all. The dive computer on my wrist started beeping a rapid ascent warning and flashing the word SLOW, SLOW, SLOW at me. The immediate imperative was to arrest the ascent. Exhaling air from my lungs, I grabbed the emergency release toggle and jerked it down. This opens up a dump valve at the highest point of the buoyancy vest. The air exploded outwards. Having dumped all the air, gravity took control again and I began to descend once more. I kicked sideways to get out of the upwelling and was able to conduct a controlled ascent.

But the currents had thrown another joker in the pack. The wall, which had always been a metre or two in front of me, had receded into the gloom as another current swept me out to sea. Five of us had entered the water. I could not see any of them. The currents had played cat and mouse with us, tossing us around, and I had no idea where any of the others were.

Angling my body across the direction of the current rather than swimming against it, I forced my way to where I guessed it would be less severe and escaped from the outward flow. The wall emerged from the gloom again. I found a ledge and slung out my reef hook. This was a time to hang on, resting and reflecting on the rapidity and power of events, allowing my breathing to get back to normal, wondering where the others were. I gazed around and above me. No one. Only fish.

The procedure when you get separated from the group is to wait for one minute and then ascend, do a safety stop at five metres for three minutes, put up a surface marker buoy to let the boat crew see where you are, and then proceed to the surface. Just before ascending to do my safety stop, I saw two columns of bubbles in the gloom reflecting some sunlight. Someone was out there in the deep, pushing to get closer to the wall. The dark forms of two divers took shape, Larry from the USA and Philipp, my friend from Germany. We re-grouped, exchanged 'okay' signals and made our way up the wall to a gentle slope. Hooked on to the rocks, we lay side by side completing our safety stop, and after three minutes made our way to the surface. The boat was about 100 metres off and came over to pick us up.

Our guide and the other missing diver were already on board. They had been swept outwards and aborted the dive after only 19 minutes. We had logged 33 minutes in what had been one of the most exciting and challenging dives any of us had experienced. Larry, who lives in the Philippines and had dived that site many times before, shook his head in disbelief.

"I have experienced strong currents there before, but never anything like that." But this was a spring tide, just after the full moon, and at three hours between high and low water the current is at its strongest. Then he giggled, "Anyone fancy another dive there?"

"You bet!" I retorted. "But in another couple of days when the moon has waned a bit and the current is less ferocious."

We did do it again, twice.

Three days later, it was almost impossible to believe it was the same place. The current was gentle, visibility was clear, and that wall had the wow factor, right enough. A riot of colour, it was teeming with fish, big and small. It was a diver's dream. The first dive had been more of a nightmare!

The best dive from a photographic point of view was the night dive at Padre Burgos Pier. On certain nights of the week it is reserved for divers between 6 and 9 p.m. It was teeming with life. Living among the piles supporting the pier were at least two different kinds of seahorse, frogfish, various pipefish, stonefish, lionfish, sea scorpions, shrimps, brittle stars, crabs, sea slugs. Almost buried in the sandy bottom lay the patient jaws of snake eels and stargazers, eyes and mouth upwards, just waiting for a tasty meal to swim past and be snapped up. It was a delightful 75 minutes of diving by torchlight, and never more than about 50 metres from the shore.

Peter's Dive Resort on Leyte provided a very pleasant week's diving with three dives each day. The food was good too. They even offered porridge for breakfast, although I had to add the salt myself. Are the Scots the only ones in the world who add a little salt to their porridge at the cooking stage to enhance the flavour? How the rest of the world can eat it without salt beats me. Without salt it is like wallpaper paste, or so I would imagine, as I have never tried to eat wallpaper paste.

On our arrival at the resort, a Filipino boy took us to our beach bungalow, and with a flourish of his arm he indicated the large double bed. "Nice big bed. Good for honeymoon." He smiled knowingly, eyes flashing. I scowled back at him.

"Aye, maybe so," I growled, "but if I wanted a honeymoon I would have an attractive lady with me! I like my friend, but a honeymoon with him was not part of the plan. I ordered a room with twin beds."

"Oh, I am so sorry," he apologised. "I thought it was a couple the room was booked for." They are very tolerant of homosexuality in the Philippines. It was no problem to pull the bed apart as it was two single beds clipped together.

As the boy split the bed into two singles, I grunted at Philipp, "Huh. Why couldn't you have been an attractive young lady?"

Chapter 6

QUE SERA SERA

A tiny piece of grit that found its way into the watertight seal of my underwater camera housing was enough to flood my camera. Salt water and electronic equipment don't like each other. I felt like a part of me was missing when diving without a camera, but it was insured and I managed to get a replacement. Until the new one arrived I had to seek something else to absorb my attention. And that is not difficult in a crazy country like the Philippines.

Friends at home had heard on TV news that Mount Mayon, the most active volcano in the Philippines, was on the verge of a major eruption and assumed that I would be there. I assured them that I was *not* sitting on its slopes with my usual lack of common-sense (Am I growing up at last?), waiting for the lava or pyroclastic flows characteristic of its recent eruptions to come sweeping down and engulf me. I was at least 500 kilometres to the south. Mind you, I admit to harbouring a desire to be there. If only there had been a direct flight!

While around 30,000 people had been evacuated from its environs by the government, more were pouring into the area to see the fireworks. An enterprising landowner built a special viewing platform to accommodate them. There's something delightfully subversive about that. Volcanic tourism was booming and brought much more income into the area than would be spent by the government on relief for those evacuated, so it was not all gloom and doom. That's life in the Philippines for you.

Nothing seems 'proper' here. How about teaching your girlfriend to drive a car on an airport runway, while an aircraft with 120 passengers on board is making its final approach? A young man had his girlfriend drive out of the jungle (the airport had no perimeter fence) and on to the runway as the plane was about to touch down. The pilot aborted the landing and the first indication the couple had that the plane was there was when it roared overhead on full throttle.

Few seem to bother with the rules of the road either. Driving a motor bike means you can dodge through dense traffic, drive on the wrong side of the road, ride up on the pavements and scatter pedestrians in a happy-go-lucky, swashbuckling manner. Anything goes. It is a liberating experience.

One-way streets? I was enjoying the friendly waves and shouts of the other bikers and the ubiquitous motorcycle trike drivers as they passed me on both sides. I am accustomed to people recognising me and calling me in a friendly manner when I return to these islands, but that day everyone seemed to be welcoming me. It was only when I reached an intersection and had to slow down to cross the path of the oncoming traffic that I heard, "ONE WAY STREET!" being shouted at me by a Filipino driver. It never struck me as odd that the oncoming traffic should be passing me on both sides of the street as I cleaved my way through the middle of them. Mayhem is normal.

With Filipinos being of relatively slight build, you can easily cram twenty or more inside a jeepney, but more people means more money. The bodywork is cleverly constructed with additional hand and footholds on the exterior, with a ladder to allow access to the roof, so they can pile on even more, sitting on the roof and hanging from the sides. They never refuse a customer. And if one or two roll off, well, Filipinos are light-weight, resilient people and bounce well.

The bus will wait for them to climb back on, laughing as they wipe the roadside dust from the grazes on arms and legs.

Health and safety regulations? Welders work without a face mask, grinders smooth welds without eye protection. Protective footwear? Steel workers handling heavy bars of steel, builders handling concrete blocks, blacksmiths at the anvil knocking sparks off hot metal, all wear the standard industrial footwear – flip flops!

At the other extremity, bureaucracy in the Philippines stretches the meaning of frustration beyond its limits. When I applied for a visa extension I had to fill in a form, show my passport, provide a photocopy of it, pay a fee, and get the passport stamped. Simple. Aye… right.

I had that efficient experience once on Boracay, but a year later when I applied for an extension in Dumaguete, the application form was read by a clerk, the passport and the passport photocopy scrutinised, and the money counted. She then passed it to another clerk who, *in her own good time*, counted the money again and also checked the form, the passport and the photocopy. She then signed the form and passed it back to the first clerk who, *in her own good time*, (and if 12 o'clock comes within that good time she will have to stop for her lunch break) picked it up and took it to where the big boss sat at his computer. In *his* own good time, he checked the form, the passport, the passport copy again, counted the money a third time, and scanned the passport through the computer to see if I had been found guilty of anything nasty such as a crime of 'moral turpitude', as it says on the immigration form you have to fill in if you ever fly to the USA.

What on earth is moral turpitude? I had never seen the word turpitude until I flew into the USA. What would a non-English speaker make of it? Same as me I suppose, just tick the No box and hope that the computer doesn't know too much about you. And who would confess to having been found guilty of a crime of moral turpitude on the flight path down to New York when the form says you will not be allowed into the country if you tick the Yes box? It's a bit late to find out then! Crazy bureaucracy is not only confined to the Philippines, but let's get back to the Philippines again.

The computer did not find me guilty of any act of moral turpitude, and churned out a letter; two copies, one for me, one for the boss man. That told us I was not on any black list, at least as far as the Philippines authorities knew, and that I could stay for another two months.

He put that letter together with the form, the passport, the copy of the passport, and the money, back on the pile of papers waiting for the second clerk who, *in her own good time*, came into his office and picked them all up. She also read that I was morally non-turpitudinal and therefore acceptable as a guest in the Philippines for a while longer, and passed it to the first clerk who, *in her own good time* (and I was now sweating, watching the hands on that clock ticking ever nearer 12 noon), was allowed at last to stamp the passport and the accompanying documents, and put the money in the cash box. She passed me my passport with the visa extension inserted with only seconds to spare before the clock struck 12. I walked past the next applicant with a smug look on my face as his shoulders sagged and he was told to come back at 2 p.m.

With a bit of common sense, one person could do the job in about two minutes: read form, scan passport, count money, stamp documents. Done. But hey, this keeps three Filipinos in a job. And it keeps the applicant waiting for at least an hour or so, unless the lunch break intervenes, and then you have to come back in the afternoon.

After another two months you have to go through it all again, if you want to stay longer. You can't beat the system. You do as the Filpinos do.

Shrug and say, *Que sera sera.*

Chapter 7
SOMETIMES

Sometimes things go wrong. In the space of only three weeks I had flooded my underwater camera, taken my mobile phone diving with me (How is that for stupidity? Phones don't like that very much, so it died too), and broken the strap fittings on my new bi-focal face-mask while diving at Siquijor, an island with strong traditions of sorcery and witchcraft. I wondered if I had offended someone and been cursed.

The mishaps continued.

I woke up with a fever, body aching, typical flu symptoms. That laid me low for a week.

Then I broke a tooth. The remaining stump proved to be difficult to remove, and after 50 minutes of pushing, pulling, wrenching, cutting part of the gum away and grinding off some bone to get at the curled up root, the dentist heaved a sigh of relief. So did I. I leaned forward to wash out my mouth. Blood poured out of my nose. It was not a nose bleed. The blood was coming from the tooth cavity, flowing up through the sinus into which the tooth root had been embedded. When the root was extracted it had left a hole in the sinus – and that created some interesting problems.

When drinking a glass of beer, the pressure of swallowing forced the beer up into the sinus, from where it flowed into the nose, ran down the nose, over my lips, and into the glass again. I was drinking recycled beer. There was a bright side to that. I could make one glass of beer last all night.

The downside was that I was beached, no diving till the hole had healed up.

This enforced break from underwater exploration encouraged me to do some exploring on land. I had never investigated the hinterland of Mindoro, an island with few large centres of population. In the mountainous northern part of the island there is little in the way of coastal plain settlements. Deep river gullies carve their way into the jungle-clad mountains. Apart from the coastal highway, there were only a few rough, dirt roads entering some of the mountain valleys for a mile or two. I travelled up one of these tracks. It shrank to become a footpath that forded rivers at various points. The only vehicles using it were buffalo carts. A hanging bridge suspended over the river connected a conventional Filipino village on one side with a Mangyan village on the other.

These valleys are home to the Mangyan people. Mangyan is the generic name for eight indigenous groups living on Mindoro, each with its own tribal name, language, and customs. The population has been estimated at around 100,000, but no official statistics are available because of the difficulties of counting remote and reclusive tribal groups, many of which have little or no contact with the outside world. They live off the land, planting sweet potato, upland rice, and taro. They trap small animals and wild pig, and the forest provides fruits and coconuts in abundance. Those who live near lowland Filipino settlements sell bananas, ginger, and wild honey. Only around 10% have embraced Christianity, despite over 400 years of Spanish and American colonisation before the Philippines gained independence in 1946.

The Mangyan people here are not as reclusive as those further up the valleys, and their way of life has been modified. Their village has been provided with rows of concrete houses, each measuring 5 metres by 4 metres, painted in bright colours, in contrast to the vernacular bamboo and thatch huts. These houses bring sanitation to people accustomed to using the forest for disposing body waste. They also have a modern elementary school.

Few people are to be seen. They drift into their homes until you have passed. The people you see at a distance look the same as the lowland Filipinos, but in the wilder areas they wear only loincloths, the children often nothing at all, and reputedly get aggressive if they see someone pointing a camera at them. My guide refused to go beyond the more civilised village.

It is hard to conceive of such a way of life only a few miles from TV, telephones, computers, and motor vehicles. They have all they need to survive, albeit in a manner we may regard as inconceivable. Food is not a problem; the forest provides. Girls are often pregnant soon after puberty and may have numerous offspring throughout their fertile years. There are no statistics regarding life expectancy, but it may be low. Medical care is confined to bush medicine. I wondered what they do when they have toothache.

Teeth are handy things to have, not just for eating, but also to grip the mouthpiece of your diving regulator. After my recent extraction that had become a problem. Being of a rather impatient nature, I gnash my teeth when frustration builds up. Well, maybe I gnashed those teeth too much. I had a lower jaw denture, but it had cracked after only ten months of use. It was repaired just before I left home, but it broke only ten days later. I could still wear it, but as one of the anchor points had broken right off, whenever I tried to eat, it jumped about all over the place, biting me. It was only of cosmetic value, allowing me a personable aspect when I smiled. That may be debatable, but I try to maintain a positive outlook and smiling helps. Sometimes. But not for long.

Dr Jonna de Chavez-Lopez, my charming Filipina dentist had the answer. New dentures were made and fitted within twelve days of the initial consultation. An excellent dentist, she has customers coming all the way from Australia and the USA for treatment. An enterprising travel agent in Brisbane saw potential in marketing dental holidays to the Philippines. Flights, hotel, and dental treatment with Dr Jonna was apparently cheaper than the price of dental treatment alone in Australia. And you can fit in some diving at the same time. Not a bad deal!

When she fitted the new teeth and gave me a mirror to see the result, I had to smile. She smiled back at me, "Guapo!" Handsome. And that made me smile even more.

Armed with my new teeth and my guapo smile, I flew off to dive at El Nido, Palawan Island. But my run of bad luck was not over yet. Food poisoning at El Nido drained me of all intestinal matter between 2 a.m. and mid-day. The dehydration was extreme. I was gulping water by the gallon, and for several hours it was all passing through the intestine, not the urinary tract. At least it flushed everything out. It was not until after mid-day that I had a pee, a signal that the body was on the road to recovery.

The accompanying symptoms: a thumping headache, raging temperature, body aches, and nausea were so powerful it was a struggle to get to the toilet without fainting. I crawled to stop the blood draining from my head. But it was the dehydration that was so worrying. After almost four days of starvation (the body simply refused food), medication, and a diet of water, I was on the way to recovery.

El Nido and its diving was one of two attractions that lured me to Palawan. The other was the famous underground river, another of the *three* eighth wonders of the world boasted by the Philippines Tourist Industry. This river winds its way for over 8 kilometres underneath the limestone hills of Palawan and is a world heritage site due to its unique biodiversity. Boats take you from a jetty at the village to the next bay where the river flows out of the cavern and into the sea. Here you transfer into small outrigger canoes equipped with large torches powered by car batteries, paddled by one man who acts as guide for exploration of the cavern. The entrance is low and narrow, but it opens out into a massive and impressive chamber likened to the dome of St Paul's Cathedral in London by one of the early English explorers here.

Another interesting feature was a small restaurant that had 'Fresh Woodworm' on the menu. I went in to try this local delicacy, a large worm that eats wood and can be found in dead trees in the mangrove swamps. However, you have to order in advance and someone goes hunting and brings the worms to you, still wriggling, but I didn't have time to wait.

El Nido

El Nido is a picturesque village hugging the shore of Bacuit Bay in northwest Palawan, an island with the most spectacular scenery in the Philippines. Towering limestone cliffs rise from the sea. Islands, which at first glance appear to have no landing places, only sheer vertical walls, suddenly reveal small hidden bays and lagoons locked within fortress-like cliffs. These cliffs have been eroded by rain into some grotesque shapes, some like cathedral spires.

Having become popular with divers and tourists, the nature of the village changed. What had been a cluster of bamboo and thatch huts along the shore became a bustling village of concrete roads and tourist accommodation, varying from very cheap to very expensive. Yet it only has an electricity supply between 5 p.m. and 2 a.m.

Getting there can be a wee bit of a challenge. The choice is between a 30-hour ferry trip from Manila, a flight to El Nido from Manila (expensive because only small planes can land on its airstrip), or flying to Puerto Princesa, the island's capital, about 240 km to the south. Most of the road north from there was a dirt road at that time.

I chose that route, but the choice was then between a 7-hour journey by air-conditioned mini-bus packed with people, or an even longer, but cheaper, journey by bus, probably also packed with people, and who knows what else. The bus had no air-conditioning. It had no windows either, so you get a blast of air, but you also get covered in fine road dust. Even in the air-conditioned minibus this was an uncomfortable journey. The driver seemed to want to get the agony over as quickly as possible and drove at high speed over the most rough and rocky parts of the road, a real bone-shaker of a ride. And then we had a puncture. The tyre had no tread left and was chewed up by the rocky road.

On the way back south, the vehicle bounced around so much that the rope tying down the luggage on the roof rack worked its way loose and a rucksack was tossed overboard. It was only several miles further on that the driver became aware of this when he got a phone call telling him that a bag had been found on the road and they were checking all the drivers to see who had lost one. The bag contained a laptop computer, mobile phone and passport, so you can imagine the look on the owner's face when he discovered it was his bag that had jumped ship several miles back. Travelling in the Philippines is never dull.

I had debated for a time which method to use, bus or minibus. I asked the receptionist at the hotel in Puerto Princesa what time the bus left. She looked vague.

"Maybe... 6 a.m,?... or 7 a.m.?... or 8 a.m.?"

"Maybe? Is there not a scheduled time of departure?"

"Well, sort of, but the bus waits till it fills up with enough people to make it worthwhile going, so sometimes the 6 o'clock bus may not go till about 7, if there are enough people on it by then, or sometimes maybe even 8 o'clock. You just have to wait till the driver decides when to go. I think it would be better for you to take the minibus. I can book it for you and it will pick you up here at the hotel. If you take the bus you need to hire a trike to take you to the bus terminal. But that is on the other side of the city, and then you have to wait till the bus driver decides to leave. Minibus is better."

I am not a good waiter.

"Okay. Book me a seat on the minibus. What time will it be here?"

"Maybe... 6.30 a.m.? or 7 a.m.? or...." She shrugged.

"Okay. I get the picture, but at least I will be sitting here waiting for it – and you are sure it will come?"

"Oh yes. It always comes... sometimes.

Chapter 8

TIDE OF FORTUNE

I enjoy live-aboard diving trips. The excellent food (and plenty of it), the chance to do four, sometimes five, dives per day in exciting environments, and the camaraderie that develops among divers makes these trips memorable. My second visit to Coron was on Oceanic Explorer, one of the Philippines-based Expedition Fleet who run live-aboard vessels in various parts of the Western Pacific. As well as exploring the wrecks of the Japanese fleet of supply vessels sunk at Coron in September 1944, the voyage included diving at Apo Reef, en route.

Unlike all my other live-aboard experiences, this trip was spoiled by serious shortcomings. The engineers could not adjust the icy blast of air that masqueraded as air-conditioning in my cabin. I was moved from my blast-freezer style cabin with hot water on tap, to one in which the air-conditioning was adjustable, but the hot water system had failed. Even in tropical waters you lose much body heat with repetitive diving, and a hot shower afterwards is important to warm up your core and restore a feeling of well-being. On this ship, all they could muster was a kettle of water that gave me two inches of boiling water in the bottom of a bucket! After adding some cold water to get it to a tolerable temperature it became three inches for washing after dives – not quite the standard expected from advertising that boasted air-conditioned cabins and hot showers.

The initial briefing left much to be desired. Safety procedures were not mentioned. Dive times were seldom adhered to. A group of Russians seemed incapable of getting ready in time for each dive, and the divemasters sat around waiting for them instead of hurrying them on. I got fed up with this nonsense and started hounding the divemasters to chase them up. Two small fast boats took the divers to position us over the wrecks. Our guide was new to the area and did not know where to go, so we were dependent on the guide in the other boat (the one with the Russians) to find the wrecks. One afternoon, the Russians were still sitting smoking, making no effort to get ready for the dive. Our group were sitting in the boat waiting, 30 minutes after we should have left. I went back aboard the ship, got them stirred up, and went back to our boat.

The boats left from opposite sides of the ship, but when the Russian boat left no one came to tell us. And they had the guide who knew where to go. By the time we got moving, almost an hour after the scheduled time for the dive, they had disappeared round the headland. Our boatman and guide then decided to follow another boat we could see a long way off, heading out to the open sea. But the dive site was supposed to be in a sheltered bay. I had to tell them we were headed in the wrong direction. They could not find the wreck among the many inlets in the area, but almost added to the list of wrecks by hitting a reef at full speed. Luckily it was the skeg of the outboard engine that struck and took the blow, not the hull of the boat. We returned to the ship to get the cruise director to come and locate the wreck for us, arriving as the Russians were finishing their dive. What should have been an afternoon dive ended up as a short-time twilight dive. Light was going fast, and we were not equipped with torches for a night dive. It was a farce. And it went on and on: incompetence, bad management, changing plans at the last moment, always to suit the Russians, without any consultation with the four non-Russian divers.

Poor visibility and strong currents are common there, but the Russians complained and to please *them* the diving on wrecks was aborted – and this was advertised as a wreck-diving trip. The ship took off to let us dive some reefs instead. That did not please me. The reefs were in very poor health and had little of interest.

Any enjoyment in that voyage was spoiled by these irritations and I sent a 3500-word report to the company pointing out their failings. To make matters worse, I had also booked a trip with the same company to Tubbataha Reef, a world heritage site, but it can only be dived between March and June. My booking had never been confirmed by the company and within three days of the date of departure, I cancelled due to the lack of communication. Instead, I decided to take a flight from Manila to Dumaguete for a few days diving.

But the tide of fortune was still against me. My flight to Dumaguete was cancelled due to a technical problem with the aircraft. However, the airline put me up in a hotel, brought me back in the morning for the extra flight, and gave me a free flight on any of their routes at anytime within the next year. Fair enough. I arrived in Dumaguete at 7:45 a.m. and booked some diving for the following day, but Lady Luck was still playing nasty tricks. That night a storm blew up and the diving was cancelled. Every plan I made seemed doomed to failure.

An email from the Explorer Fleet arrived, apologising for the lack of communication. It explained that they'd had to change the dates for my Tubbataha Reef trip as they'd received a full ship group booking for my dates, but they'd forgotten to tell me. They offered me a place on the transition cruise of their flagship vessel, the Stella Maris, starting 9 March, when the boat leaves its base at Anilao and sails south for the first of its Tubbataha cruises. This transition cruise also offered diving at Apo Reef and Cuyo Island on the way south, four days at Tubbataha reef with five dives per day, and finishing at Puerto Princessa.

That sounded attractive, but I was 500 miles away at Dumaguete, with only two days left before the boat was due to sail. On receipt of my complaints about the shortcomings of the Coron Trip the previous week, they had offered some recompense, a $200 gift voucher which I could only use on their boats for gifts (who needs another T shirt or mug?), nitrox, food, or drink. Not much good if I wasn't going to be on their boats again.

I offered my own suggestion for recompense. They could fly me back, at their expense, from Dumaguete to Manila, arrange a taxi to meet me at the airport, and take me to Anilao (a two-hour drive), give me the transition cruise *free* to make up for all the inconvenience, discomfort and additional expense I had suffered as a result of their bungling and lack of communication, put me up overnight in a hotel in Puerto Princessa at the end of the cruise, and then fly me back to Dumaguete. In return, I would write a full report on the cruise for them and, if the experience proved to be a good one, I would promote the company among the diving fraternity, and in my lectures when I came home. They had already told me they wanted to use my critical report of the Coron trip in their boat operator's manual, so I offered to accept the free cruise, flights etc instead of demanding a management consultant's fee – and consultants don't come cheap! – for their use of my report.

My letter went all the way to the owner of the company, Mr John Wee. He issued orders that my demands be met in full, and I should be accommodated in a de-luxe cabin on board the Stella Maris. Furthermore, I should be given *two* nights in a hotel at Puerto Princessa because the flights from there were only operating three days per week and I would have to spend an additional night there after disembarking. The tide of fortune seemed to be flowing in my favour at last.

My arrival on board Stella Maris at Anilao as a non-paying guest proved interesting. John Wee had come down in person to meet me, and to brief the crew on my feedback from the previous fiasco. He went over my report in detail with the crew, and spelled out what was expected of them on this cruise. Axelle, one of the dive guides, told me later my report had shaken things up. She said they had been living in dread of 'this character who had made so many complaints,' but, as she put it, "It was such a surprise to meet you. You're not like that at all. You're really quite nice." They were all very keen to make sure everything was okay. Even the captain welcomed me on board in full dress uniform: brilliant whites with gold braided cap and epaulettes.

The ship left Anilao that evening and picked up five American divers, travelling as a group, from Sabang Beach on the other side of

Verde Passage. They were a great bunch with whom I have formed lasting friendships. They have joined me for diving every year since, and three of them have visited me in Scotland. Another American from California, not part of that group, had been everywhere, done everything, and found everything "*really*" interesting." A married couple from Denmark and myself were the only Europeans. The food was excellent. They even had porridge for breakfast for me.

Tubbataha Reef looked beautiful in the sunshine when we arrived; a thin strip of white sand fringed by the palest turquoise blue, giving way to the deep aquamarine of the ocean where the reef falls to the seabed over 1000 feet below. Dropping off the boat, visibility was as near perfect as it could be. White sand lay between the corals on the ledge, then that fantastic wall, encrusted with growth, dropped into the blue void. Sharks patrolled along the wall. Multi-coloured fish glided among the corals. Turtles cruised past in leisurely fashion, and you could see for miles along the reef, or so it seemed.

The star of the show was a large manta ray that cruised, quite unconcerned by our presence, right through the middle of the group. The Americans were gob-smacked by it all. "I've seen more varieties of fish on that one dive than I've seen in all the dives I've done in the Caribbean," gasped one of them when we surfaced. When asked for my impression, I replied with typical Scottish understatement, "Och, it was no' bad."

"Not Bad? How could anything be better than that?"

Tubbataha consists of two atolls, about five miles apart, their coral reefs encrusting the tops of ancient undersea volcanoes. There is little to be seen above the surface: on each atoll only one small hump of sand with a handful of palm trees, a few lumps of coral showing at low tide, and a long white strip of sand washed by the sea. A ranger station, manned by armed guards, is perched on stilts. They are there to protect the reef from the predations of illegal fishing. One dive revealed evidence of the devastation caused by dynamite fishing.

This invidious method of fishing is practised in several parts of South East Asia. It destroys the source of food and the provider of shelter for immature fish and other marine animals. Corals may be hard, but are brittle; some are soft, tender, plant-like growths. Neither can survive the shock of a dynamite explosion.

Once the shelter and food source has been destroyed, the reef lies shattered into millions of pieces. What was once a Garden of Eden, becomes a wasteland of rubble offering no food, no shelter. No living coral equals no fish. No fish equals no livelihood. The easy catch is a one-off event, killing the source of food and income for at least a generation. While nature has a wonderful way of regenerating, a coral reef is a living, growing structure that has taken thousands, or even millions, of years to develop, but it can be destroyed in seconds.

The reef was honeycombed with caves and tunnels. I found one cave at a low level and looked in. A bluish light ahead signified that it had another opening higher up. I decided to explore. In the dark recesses, I looked up what was like a chimney. Floating upwards through this vertical passage to the daylight, I emerged at a small opening, just large enough for one diver to pass through. Axelle had been taking the role of tail-end-charlie to mop up any strays who may have been left behind the group. She hadn't noticed that I had slipped into the cave about five metres below and she timed it to perfection to turn and look at the hole just as my head appeared, framed in the opening. That startled her!

"How did you get in there?" she demanded when we surfaced, "I thought you were way ahead of me. I thought I was seeing an apparition. It was like having a dream…no…more like a nightmare!" Girls know how to put a guy down.

My encounters with the explorer fleet had a happy ending and I submitted a positive report to Mr Wee. I didn't have to pay anything, not for drinks on board, or nitrox, or national park fees. That made amends for my previous bad experience. The company deserve credit for that. My luck had changed at last – or was it luck?

While trekking in the Patagonian mountains, an American in our group had given me a book. It discussed why some people seem to be lucky, while others appear to be unlucky in life. The book's thesis was that so-called lucky people *make* their own good fortune by the decisions they make, and in particular by how they react to situations: keep cool, stay positive and always look for a win-win outcome. He thought I should read it, as he felt my life seemed to be just such a case study.

It certainly seemed to apply in this case.

Chapter 9
WELCOME TO JAKARTA

Some places hit you like a slap on the face, or a sensuous kiss from a beautiful stranger. You haven't met such beautiful strangers? Okay, but it happens to me all the time, especially when I wear my kilt! That's how Java hit me: an island that has left indelible images in my mind, aroused my emotions, and given me that inward glow when I am surrounded by warm-hearted, amiable people.

As the plane murmured its way over a flat, low-lying, and very wet landscape towards Jakarta airport, it looked very much like the approach to Amsterdam. Scattered around this flat-as-a-pancake, rural landscape were small houses and farm buildings, red brick-built, with red pan-tiled roofs. I found that surprising in the tropics where you become accustomed to a vernacular rural architecture of bamboo and thatch, but Java was a Dutch colony for a long time and the colonial influence lingers on in its architecture. Dotted around the landscape were several lakes and what looked like canals, but as the plane lost height I could see that it wasn't boats ploughing their way through the water: it was cars and trucks. These 'canals' were flooded roads.

The area had experienced heavy rainfall over the previous twenty-four hours. The road from the airport into the city was a river, with cars pushing through water up to their floor boards, even deeper in some places. A journey that normally takes about one hour took three.

Jakarta city centre was in chaos, with flooding so deep that traffic could not navigate through some parts of the city. Policemen, knee deep in water, with trouser legs rolled up, diverted traffic. At other places, the local residents in the middle of the road performed a useful service to motorists by directing cars away from the deeper areas, and controlled the merging of lines of traffic as three lanes were forced by the depth of water into one passable lane due to the camber of the road on some bends. Often up to their mid-thighs in water, they seemed to be enjoying it all and looked very self-important as their hands flailed about in the air, holding lines of traffic up, then guiding them to safety. Without doubt, they were important!

I don't know what Jakarta would be like in normal conditions, but on this occasion its traffic was in a state of total anarchy. Cars drove down one-way streets the wrong way, ignored red lights, executed U-turns in traffic that was already grid-locked, creating more mayhem as they sought an alternative route. Some drove along the motorway in the wrong lane. They put on their flashing indicators, flashed their headlights, and the opposing traffic dodged out of their way. It was mayhem. It may have taken me three hours to get to my hotel from the airport, but it was enthralling entertainment, and more than just a little exciting.

And the people? Despite being flooded out of their homes, they seemed to be having fun, wading about, laughing, talking as they met others, and the children played in the floodwater.

My taxi, a 4-wheel drive Toyota Landcruiser, had no trouble navigating the waters. The locals, noticing a white face gazing at them from the open window, waved to me. The welcome in their smiles, despite the misery of their plight, generated an affection for this dirty, muddy, rain-soaked, crazy, chaotic city. The population may be 20 million or so, but no one knows for sure. It is constantly changing as people come and go from the rural hinterland. Jakarta, a seething, often under-nourished mass of humanity, many of whom live in appalling conditions, struck me as a place with a warm heart.

Those who lived along the riverbanks had it worst of all. Often living in squatter shacks, made up of whatever material they could find: wood, tarpaulin, corrugated iron, with roofs not nailed down, but weighted down by old tyres, lumps of concrete, heavy planks of wood or scrap iron, they waded about up to their waists in water, in some places up to their necks. Homes were awash as the muddy-brown flood surged through narrow alleyways, sweeping away the few possessions they had, and sometimes entire houses.

Welcome to Jakarta

The following day moved me deeply. I arrived at the station for what should have been a three-hour train journey, followed by a seven-hour bus journey. The train was due to leave at 8.20 a.m., but it didn't arrive until 11.30 a.m. It crawled through Jakarta, stopping frequently for signals to allow trains coming from the opposite direction to make passage into the city. Sometimes we waited for over an hour, before getting the green light to proceed. There had been more torrential rain during the night, and not long after the train left the station we entered the flood zone. The railway was on an embankment, keeping us well above the water level in most places, but when crossing some bridges, the tracks were submerged. Only the girders supporting the sides of the bridges confirmed that there was still a bridge there.

The high viewpoint of the train offered unforgettable sights. Large areas of the city were engulfed by water so deep that you could only see the roofs of the flimsy, single-storey houses. Some walls had already collapsed, leaving tin roofs flapping in the surge of water. Tables, sofas, armchairs floated along, bouncing from wall to wall along the rivers that had once been streets.

People waded in and out of houses trying to salvage what they could, carrying bundles of clothing and other possessions high above their heads. Ropes had been slung across the deeper water from the houses to the railway embankment, so that refugees from the flood could haul themselves along the ropes to the safety of the higher ground. Some enterprising lads had obtained inflated tyre inner tubes to act as rescue vehicles for women and children who were being ferried across the raging floods, clinging to the rope to stop themselves being swept away. The looks of relief and the cheers from the neighbours as a young mother, in a rubber tube, cradling a tiny baby in her arms, was hauled across the fast flowing waters to reach the safety of the railway embankment will remain forever in my mind.

People in taller houses were confined to their upper floors. On many of the single storey houses they sat on the roofs, hoping that the floods would come no higher. A few military inflatable boats paddled around, helping terrified grannies, mothers, and tearful young children from their precarious perches on shaky roofs, into the rubber boats.

The most amazing thing of all was that, among the thousands of homeless people who had sought refuge on the railway embankment, there was little evidence of misery. As the train crawled through the hordes of refugees, I took photographs at an open door. They don't bother to close the doors of the train – that is the air conditioning in economy class carriages! They waved at me and shouted, "Welcome to Jakarta!" They smiled, laughed, and posed for pictures for me. They cheered when people made it across to the safe ground. They laughed when people fell in. They splashed each other with the brown water. They were enjoying this as much as we do when we get a good fall of snow. Whatever will be, will be, and let's enjoy life, seemed to be the philosophy. It was a moving experience.

It took three hours just to get to the city boundaries. Arriving at Bandung more than six hours late, we still faced a seven-hour bus journey to Pangandaran, our destination for that night. It was now 7 p.m. and the last bus had left. Our tour guide, living up to the name of the company, Intrepid, left us at the station and disappeared for a while. He negotiated a deal with a minibus driver and all we had to pay was an additional 10,000 rupiah per head. It sounds a lot, but it was only worth about 65 UK pence or $1 US at that time. With an air-conditioned minibus for our exclusive use, we did the journey in five hours instead of seven, arriving just after mid-night.

On arrival at the hotel in Pangandaran, we learned that we had been lucky. Our train was the last one to leave the city before the railway embankment collapsed due to flood erosion.

Chapter 10

WHAT EARTHQUAKE?

Pangandaran, a pleasant seaside town on Java's south coast, had the douce atmosphere of a middle-class British holiday resort. However, less than a year before, its tranquility had been shattered by an offshore earthquake that created a tsunami that swept over the south coast of Java. Houses and hotels fronting the beach stood forlorn with sea-facing walls stove in, and roofs sagging. Some were demolished, a sad pile of rubble reminding us that this was once a home. Small fishing boats had been swept into the jungle, some smashed to pieces against trees, others perched high on massive tree boughs. Over 1000 victims lie buried in the town's cemetery, evidence of the awesome forces of nature.

But life goes on. An open-air fund-raising concert along the seafront attracted my attention. Having the only white face in the crowd, I stood out as a stranger. Well, maybe the kilt had something to do with it as well. A man approached me and introduced himself. As the singer started to belt out a lively song he grabbed my hand and said, "Come, you are dancing with me."

Now, where I come from, dancing with a *man* is not the sort of game I play. We are a wee bit conservative about that kind of thing in the highlands of Scotland. However, as I protested, a host of other men filled the space between the audience and the stage and started gyrating to the sounds of the singer's lusty voice. All the local men seemed to have no problem with it, so I might as well go with the flow and started swinging my kilt with the rest of them. The ladies all sat and smiled their approval. When I threw in some Cook Island warrior dancing, that created a stir. Cameras clicked, and a guy with a TV camera crept up to film the action.

It surprised me that all the dancers up to that point were men. Usually it's the females who are uninhibited about dancing and get up first, but in this Muslim society the women sat watching the men – until they saw what was happening. Then a group of them got up, elbowed my male partner out of the way, and insisted I dance with them. It looked as if I had been a catalyst in stirring up a women's emancipation movement in a Muslim society. Would the men seize me, flog me, or stone me to death for inciting this revolution? But no, this was all good fun, and more was to come.

When the song ended, I walked off, but the singer roared at me through her mike, "Hey Papa, don't go. Come up here and dance with me." I shook my head. The crowd cheered their encouragement. My male partner grabbed me and started to hoist my leg up on to the stage. Again, I had to go with the flow. The singer faced me, and in an excellent imitation of Tina Turner, rasped out a raunchy number, thrusting her hips at me provocatively. I can play that game too, and with a few provocative thrusts of my own, the crowd cheered and clapped. And the TV cameraman was capturing it all on video.

Next day, I went into the internet café. Some boys sitting there gasped and pointed at me, and then at the monitor screens. "It's him!" Sure enough, there I was on the screen dancing on the stage. They'd obtained a copy of the video of the concert. My dancing in the kilt was raising funds for those who had been rendered homeless by the tsunami. I had become a celebrity.

Pangandaran provided the opportunity to get into the jungle and meet some of its inhabitants: macaque monkeys, deer, scorpions, flying foxes. Our guide demonstrated how to 'fish' for scorpions. Squatting beside a hole at the base of a rotting tree trunk, he dangled a string with small strip of chicken on the end of it into the hole. Within a few seconds the string twitched. He gave a yank and hauled out a hungry scorpion clinging to the piece of chicken. He already had a twig by his side and used it to pin the claws to the ground. The sting at the end of the tail curled up to strike, but the hand holding the twig over the claws was out of reach. From behind, he seized the tail between the thumb and forefinger of his other hand so that the sting was also now immobilised. Putting his foot over the end of the twig, he squeezed the trapped claws together with his right hand, released the twig from under his foot, and lifted the scorpion up. Easy. When you know how!

Green Canyon, a deep, stalactite-dripping cleft in limestone rock in the jungle, had a Jurassic Park feel to it. Journeying through it by boat as far as a waterfall, we hooked up to a rock beside the falls, stripped off, and dived in. Cooling and invigorating after the steamy heat of the jungle, we swam downriver in the powerful current, dodging rocks, swirling in eddies. We were showered by waterfalls that tumbled through the narrow slit in what, at one part, is almost a cave where both sides of the canyon are so close you could almost step over it. Monitor lizards gazed at us from rocky perches. The opaque, muddy-brown waters made it impossible to see underwater and this lack of visibility created a sense of insecurity. It was impossible to see any rocks that might lurk under the surface, or to know if there might be something nasty lurking down there. However, our guide assured us that there were no crocodiles, and it proved to be a refreshing and exhilarating experience.

Yogyakarta, a sprawling city in central Java, was an eight-hour hour bus journey away. Yogya's main tourist attractions are the Sultan's Palace, the extraordinary Prambanan Hindu temple, constructed in the 10th century, but cordoned off as a result of earthquake damage the previous May, and at nearby Magelang, the remarkable 9th century Buddhist monument of Borobudur, the decline of which is dated to the 14th century when Java became Islamic. Yogya also provided an opportunity to see the ancient Indian legend of Ramayana, portrayed in music and dance in an open-air theatre, a colourful and spectacular event. Culture, palaces, and temples are fine, but two days in a city is more than enough for me. I went to bed looking forward to getting up the jungle again next day, and climbing Mount Bromo, an active volcano, the day after. That is more my kind of thing. This place was too quiet for my liking.

Borobudur

The earthquake struck at 2:30 a.m.

Only a few months before, Yogya had been hit by an earthquake that took 5,782 lives; 36,299 people were injured, and 135,000 houses damaged. An estimated 1.5 million people were left homeless. The evidence was everywhere. Like a city that had been bombed, rows of houses were punctuated by gaps piled with the rubble that once had been homes where people had lived and died. Temple walls had been cracked, some leaning perilously, and roofs had caved in. Traumatised by that recent event, this latest quake caused the population of Yogya some concern. Some earthquakes produce a sideways shaking effect. This time the vibration was mainly vertical, an up-and-down movement of the earth's crust, shaking people awake in their beds, and when they stood on the floor they were bouncing up and down. Ornaments danced on shelves. Parents hauled their children out of their beds to relative safety outside, with fearful faces traumatised by the memory of the last quake only months before.

However, measuring 4.2 on the Richter scale, this was only a mild earthquake. It was big enough to shock, but not strong enough to damage or kill, and after waiting to feel confident that no more tremors were imminent, people returned indoors to try to sleep. It was the talk of the town next day. Everywhere, people discussed how terrified they had been, how the children had been crying, how they couldn't sleep afterwards for fear of another tremor. And always they asked me, "How did you feel? Were you terrified?"

My answer was always an honest, "No, not at all." The truth is that if they hadn't been so keen to talk about it I wouldn't have been able to tell you all this, for I had slept through the whole thing.

As I said before, this place was too quiet for me.

The journey by bus from Yogyakarta to the Seloliman Nature Reserve, nestling in the foothills of the mountain range that spans Java from east to west, took all of ten hours. Nine months earlier it would have taken much less than that. We encountered several detours along the way as a result of another type of eruption. The problem this time was mud, pouring out of the biggest mud volcano in the world. It was created by the blowout of a natural gas well. Gas and hot mud started spewing from the well on May 28, 2006, when the drill penetrated a layer of liquid sediment. Attempts to pump concrete down the well failed to stop the flow. The drilling company speculated that the earthquake that struck Yogyakarta on May 27, the day before the well erupted, might have cracked the ground, creating pathways for the mud to reach the surface, but other reports suggested that the drilling procedure was faulty. At its peak, 180,000 cubic metres of mud were spewing out daily. Barriers built to contain the mud failed and it wiped out 12 villages, killed 13 people, and displaced more than 42,000.

More effective levees have now been erected to contain it in a huge lake covering an area of 7 square kilometres and 20 metres deep, and it is is now visible from space. Geologists said it may be impossible to stop, but flow rates had reduced to around 10,000 cubic metres per day. All attempts to plug the geyser failed, new spouts were opening up, and there were indications that the void created by the loss of so much material has weakened the geological structure, with evidence of subsidence from around 0.5 to 14 metres deep. Such subsidence could result in the formation of a caldera if the ground collapses in on itself. Meanwhile, 17 years on, the mud still flows, threatening more villages, homes, and livelihoods in the East Java district of Sidoarjo.

Although a major disaster for the people living nearby, for the scientific community it was a chance to study the evolving geological progress of a mud volcano. In the past, mud vulcanologists could only study existing or ancient mud volcanoes during dormant periods. This one has presented a unique opportunity to conduct experiments on a developing mud volcano to further scientific understanding.

The Indonesian President at the time, Susilo Bambang Yudhoyono, enraged victims who had not been compensated for their loss of property when he suggested that they should look on the bright side and develop the mud lake – that had engulfed their homes, swallowed up their land, and destroyed their livelihoods – as a tourist attraction!

Now, there's optimism for you. And a monumental lack of sensitivity!

Chapter 11

ERUPTION

J ava is the most densely populated island in the world with a population of 115 million. I expected long expanses of jungle with few inhabitants, but there are people everywhere. Houses are crowded together in the villages to avoid taking over the fertile ground which grows the rice they depend upon for survival. The overall standard of housing across Java and Bali seems to be better than in the Philippines, although the slums of Jakarta are just as squalid as those of Manila.

In the foothills of Eastern Java, the rice fields offer an attractive man-made landscape with the contours of each hill sculpted into terraces. The jungle presses in close here and the noise at night is deafening with cicadas screeching, squirrels and monkeys squabbling in the trees, and frogs croaking. Huge black beetles fly about like bombs, and this is a land of big spiders. These horrified some of our party, but they don't appear to be dangerous. I tried to persuade them that spiders should be treated kindly. They eat mosquitos which are far more dangerous. Mosquito repellent is a must for travellers in this part of the world.

After trekking through the rice paddies and jungle, we visited a large herb garden. Our guide gathered a bundle of herbs and made a brew reputed to have powerful medicinal properties. An infusion of cardamom seed, lemon grass, ginger root, cinnamon, and palm sugar, it tasted delicious. I swallowed three cups of it to ward off whatever ailments might be tempted to afflict me. Cardamom is used to treat infections of the teeth and gums, to prevent and treat throat troubles, congestion of the lungs, pulmonary tuberculosis, inflammation of eyelids, and digestive disorders. It also is used to break up kidney stones and gallstones, and as an antidote for both snake and scorpion venom. I was comforted by the assurance that my three cups of the delicious brew had me pretty well fortified against whatever illness, bites, or stings might come my way. Anything unpleasant that might get into my system would have a fight on its hands. The large herb garden here is maintained to preserve the medicinal herbs used in traditional remedies. They even had one plant alleged to have the same properties as Viagra. And in case you are wondering... no, I did not grab some of its seeds.

Vegetable fields

The next move was into the mountains; a long, uphill climb of about six thousand feet to some villages clinging to the slopes of some of Java's biggest volcanoes. The cool mountain air and fertile volcanic soil creates ideal conditions for growing vegetables in the most amazing fields I have ever seen, with plants growing in mathematically precise rows, angled in herring-bone patterns to avoid erosion by rainfall, along slopes of up to forty-five degrees. No mechanisation is possible on these slopes. Everything has to be done by hand. For mile after mile they are cultivated, presenting a beautiful patchwork of angled rows of vegetables in various shades of green: potatoes, cabbages, tomatoes, onions, and many more. It was astonishing in both the sheer scale of it, and in its aesthetic appeal.

A small hotel high up on the slopes was our resting place that night, or at least part of the night. We were aroused at 3:15 a.m. A winding journey by jeep, growling up the steep slopes of Mount Bromo, took us to a high point on the edge of a massive caldera.

Mt Bromo

Still active, Bromo had blown its conical top off a very long time ago and it fell in on itself creating this vast caldera, a huge flat-bottomed crater several miles across. From our viewpoint, the rising sun revealed a remarkable landscape. Unclothed from its veil of darkness by the early morning light, lay the vast, desert-like caldera of Bromo. The pressure of escaping gasses had created a new volcano on the floor of the caldera, successive eruptions forming a neat cone of volcanic ash which has been eroded by the rain, its sides now riven with fissures and gullies. That cone had died out, but beside it Bromo had thrown up yet another younger volcano with a vast, grey mouth out of which poured an incessant plume of white smoke.

A few miles beyond Bromo soared the towering Mount Semeru, an active volcano that has been in a state of almost constant eruption since 1967. The highest mountain in Java at around 12,000 feet, it now stood, a stark triangle silhouetted against the clear blue of the sky. And, as if to herald the dawn, it growled and blew a huge plume of brown smoke and ash, billowing up thousands of feet into the morning sky. The top of the plume flattened out in the anvil shape characteristic of a massive thunderhead, illuminated into yellow, red, and brown colours by the rising sun. Here were the primeval forces of nature at work, presenting an unforgettable image of fearsome beauty and energy.

Mount Semeru eruption

I had hoped to see a volcanic eruption, and now I had. It wasn't a magma eruption, so I missed the sight of molten lava flowing down the mountain, but the TV news that evening reported clouds of ash had settled on towns and villages downwind of the volcano. Plants were covered in grey dust, and people were seen sweeping it off their roofs.

Going down into the caldera of Mt Bromo, a desert with only a few pioneer plants colonising the volcanic ash that forms its flat floor, we arrived at the base of the new smoking vent. A steep climb up took me to the edge of its crater. Looking into an active volcano is an awe-inspiring experience. A dark hole grumbled, hissing, venting off obnoxious smelling hydrogen sulphide gas and clouds of steam. The inward slope of the crater was steep; stumble and fall into that and there would be little chance of escape.

Bromo can turn nasty. Between November 2010 and the end of January 2011 it erupted ash continuously, with associated tremors and earthquakes. Tourists were excluded from the area, and many airlines cancelled flights to Bali and Lombok as a result of the ash in the atmosphere which was reported as high as 18,000 feet. It had seriously affected visibility, and could damage aircraft engines.

Looking outward across the flat desert floor of the ancient caldera to its precipitous edges, you can only gasp at the colossal energy that must have been released when the original mountain top blew itself to smithereens and collapsed inwards to create this desert bowl several miles across. How high had Bromo been originally, I wondered, before its towering cone could no longer be sustained by its relatively weak ash-like structure. That must have made quite a bang.

I thought about neighbouring Semeru, just a few miles away, still growling and pouring ash into the atmosphere. How strong is its structure? When is it likely to collapse inwards, or explode outwards as many volcanoes do at some time, and with what devastating effect?

On the crater edge of smoking Mt Bromo, I had experienced another of the most powerful and enduring images of my journey through Java, with a sense of the immense power of nature's seismic forces and how they have shaped our world.

The final leg across east Java by train was a delight. Our group of five and a couple of Irish-born residents of Australia were the only ones with white faces on the train, so it was not surprising that we aroused some interest. As soon as I sat down, a family opposite me regarded me with some curiosity, especially a small girl about seven years old. She looked at me. I looked at her and smiled. She hid behind her book and whispered something to her mother. Her mother smiled at me and I smiled back. Her father smiled at me and I smiled back and nodded. "Selmat pagi. Apa Kabar?" My greeting, 'Good morning. How are you?' in fluent Bahasa Indonesia, impressed them and they responded, but I ran out of vocabulary after about thirty seconds. However, that was all the encouragement they needed and the questions started to roll out: "Where are you from? What is your name?" All the usual stuff.

The carriage was very hot and Yude, our Indonesian guide, then came along and told us there were empty seats in the first class, air-conditioned carriage. We could upgrade for 25,000 rupiah (about £1.50), for the extra comfort. The others went off, but I said, "Och no. I've made some friends here. I'll stick around." I'd come to savour the Indonesian way of life, and travelling in a steamy, hot train with new friends was an enjoyable part of that experience. After they got off, I stood by the carriage door which was permanently open. A blast of air blowing around my body was more refreshing and I enjoyed the pastoral scenes that flowed past me.

Each village the train passed through, and at every station, people looked up, and when they saw my white face, they waved and called out, "Welcome!" I waved to them. I felt like royalty.

Travelling by train lets you see the back yards of towns and villages, and this was no exception. Some of the poorer houses, little more than tin and plywood shanties, were so close to the track I could have shaken hands with the residents as I passed. This was a rural excursion, no big cities, just small country towns and villages, rice fields and low, rolling hills fissured by deep gorges. It also provided intimate glimpses of rural life.

Java rice terraces

Outside one village a stream flowed past a cluster of houses. It passed through an open-topped concrete structure with walls about six feet high and two separate chambers. The stream was split at the point of entry and flowed through both chambers. In one chamber three naked men were having a bath. The other chamber was for the ladies. My elevated position offered an intimate view of this aspect of community life; men and women engaging in communal bathing at the end of a day's work, but with males and females separated. One of the women crouched down, attempting to hide herself, but it was too late. It was impossible not to notice, so I plead innocent to the possible charge of voyeurism. A few minutes later, I spotted another elderly man bathing in the stream. It's the way life here.

That was the last of my enduring images of Java, an island of so many welcomes and smiling people, an island for which I had developed a real affection. But reflecting on the floods, earthquakes, eruptions, and tsunamis that are a feature of life on Java, maybe Scotland is not such a bad place to live after all.

Chapter 12

BALI

The ferry from Java to Bali took about an hour. It felt great to be on the sea again, to smell the salt air, to feel the motion of a ship on the ocean. It seemed to be caressing me, luring me to its bosom once more. It was irresistible.

I organised some diving at Menjangan Island, a small island off the northwest tip of Bali with lots of colourful coral. A day later, at Tulamben, on the northeast coast of Bali, I was diving on a wreck, the USS Liberty. Torpedoed in 1942, it was run ashore before it sank and what could be salvaged was taken from her. She was a hulk in shallow water until 1963 when a volcanic eruption coincided with an earthquake. The tremors caused her to slide down a slope, and she came to rest with her stern at 30 metres and her bow only 5 metres below the surface.

This depth range makes for an interesting dive. The marine life at 5 metres is different from that at 30 metres. It is a big ship, 395 feet long, and the pounding of the sea over many decades has broken her up, making it an easy wreck dive, and a very safe one as the current is never more than slight. I did two dives on her, the first around the exterior, and on the second dive I penetrated the structure, not that there was much penetration as it is so open now. A useless wreck for man, it has become a marine community, home to many beautiful fish, corals, sponges, and anemones. A large turtle lurked in the gloom of the forward hold. On the stern, clinging to a large Gorgonian fan coral, was a tiny pygmy sea-horse. Above and around us, an enormous school of trevally swirled in tight formation, blotting out the sunlight as it passed above us. It was a delightful dive in perfect conditions.

The gap between Bali and Lombok is a narrow channel through which a strong current flows. About a couple of miles from Padangbai, Gili Tepekong is a saw-toothed reef with two rocky islets and some black fangs sticking out of the water. It looked formidable in the big swell that drove large, breaking waves to foaming destruction on its dark crags. The Guide to Diving in Indonesia offers a cautionary note: '*a tricky dive with strong currents and powerful surges, it is one that should only be attempted by experienced divers.*' It was a challenging dive, but a very rewarding one with beautiful corals, anemones and sponges, sharks, barracuda, and a host of colourful reef fish.

Gili Tepekong

But those currents were tricky. One moment they tempt you into relaxing as they propel you along, drifting effortlessly, enjoying the panorama of colours on the reef. Then they become perverse and turn against you. One moment they drive you downwards, and a moment later thrust you upwards at an alarming rate. The big swell surges towards the reef, threatening to dash you against its rock walls, but reflected back from its collision with the rock, it sucks you off in the opposite direction, like hanging on the end of a huge pendulum. This was a dive where constant vigilance, good timing, lots of fin work, and good buoyancy control were required. It was exciting, exhilarating at times, and called on all the experience I had gained.

Bali is an island of contrasts. In the south, around the densely populated area near the airport at Denpassar, it has become commercialised, choked with traffic, and is far removed from the image of a tropical island paradise. It is a popular area with young Australians who enjoy surfing on the big waves that roll in from the ocean. Restaurants and bars abound; loud noise masquerades as music. Drunkenness among tourists is commonplace at night.

A few miles around the coast, you enter a different world in which the Balinese people grow rice, engage in fishing, or whatever their business may be. Tourism is more low-key; the towns and villages are quiet at night. At Lovina, a village on the north coast and our base for the first couple of days, the arrival of our party of five increased the number of tourists by 100%. Tertigangga and Ubud, the other two overnight stops were also quiet. These places don't attract the raucous crowds that flock to Kuta, but they offer glimpses of the Balinese way of life. They are mellow, like the Balinese people.

The tourism trade in Bali had been devastated by the infamous nightclub bombing in November 2002 at Kuta Beach, in which over 200 lives were lost. That vile act, perpetrated by Malaysian Islamic terrorists, was alien to the friendly Balinese people who suffered as their economy depends on the tourist trade. The hordes of Australians who once flocked to Bali dropped to a trickle for a year or two. Hotels, restaurants, tour operators, dive companies were all struggling, and the effect was felt right round the island. For several years, warnings were issued by the Australian government to travellers not to visit Indonesia. The governments of Britain, Canada, USA were also advising against visiting this island of friendly people. I never felt under threat at any time in Indonesia; not in the streets of Jakarta, not on Bali, nor anywhere else. I was greeted with warmth by smiling people everywhere, and never more so than on Bali. Many people I met begged me to return.

On our final night, Yude, our guide, arranged for me to play the spoons with a band at the Jazz Café in Ubud, where we had our last dinner together as a group. I had a brief audition with the boys in the band during the interval. Big smiles all round. "You're on!" was the unanimous verdict. At the end of the interval the compere announced: "Ladies and Gentlemen, tonight we have a special guest star to perform for you. Let's give a big welcome to Mr John from Scotland!" At the end of the tune I got up to leave the stage, but there was a howl of protest from the audience. "No! More! More!"

"How about it, Mr John?" asked the compere.

"Aye, no problem." I grinned and sat down again.

They played a lively Latino Jazz, most of which worked well with the spoons and, as is common in a jazz performance, each instrument gets a solo spot to improvise around the central theme. When my turn came, the other instruments were muted, playing only a few skeletal notes in the background to allow me to demonstrate my virtuosity. Playing with good musicians can lift your performance. Their skill in improvisation inspired me; creativity took over and directed my hands to make sounds I'd never produced before. My mind was working on different levels. The conscious part recognised and marvelled at what was happening, but the music itself had taken control at a different level altogether. It just happened. As the solo spot drew to a close and the rest of the band fell in behind me, picking up the tune again, the compere called out, "Mr John!" The audience clapped and roared their appreciation. That's Jazz!

Afterwards, the waiters and waitresses wanted to try their hand, and several of the audience too. "Hey, come and have a drink. I've never seen anything like that in my life." Our last night had developed into a party, at least for me.

That event ended my first Indonesian tour on a high note. I had no doubt Bali would see me again, and it did, several times, as my gateway to several of Indonesia's other wonderful diving locations.

Chapter 13

A TRAWANGAN LEGEND

"**S**top the bus! Stop the Bus! FIRE! FIRE! FIRE! Everyone out! GO! GO! GO!" shrieked a panic-stricken Frenchman as he dashed from the back of the bus to escape. The brakes went on, the bus pulled in to the side of the road, and there was a mass exodus.

The first sign that something had gone wrong was when the air-conditioning in the bus packed in, followed by an immediate rise in temperature and stuffiness. Outside, the sun was blazing hot. It must have been about 35 degrees Celsius in the shade, and under the relentless heat of the sun, the bus became an oven. Hands reached up to fiddle with the air nozzles, but to no avail. I was about to go to speak to the driver when the panicky shout came from the back of the bus and passengers rushed past me to get to the door. I looked round to see smoke billowing from under the rear seat, accompanied by the smell of burning rubber. All the others ran a long way from the bus and stood in a huddle on the roadside verge in the heat of the sun. I went round to the back of the bus with the driver. He opened the engine hatch. We both stood to the side in case there might be a sudden flash as it opened and let the air in. Thick smoke poured out. There were no flames, only sparking and smouldering around one of the battery terminals.

The high-tension lead from the battery had been bent and was in contact with a metal bracket. It had short-circuited. "Have you anything to lever it off the terminal with?" I asked. He rummaged in a tool kit and brought out a long bar and a pair of rubber gloves. When he managed to prise the lead off the terminal, the sparking and smouldering stopped. The smoke drifted away. We were stranded.

We had pulled in close to a small roadside café. The owner smiled at our misfortune. The heat of the sun encouraged passengers to buy cold drinks. Every cloud has its silver lining, if not for us, then for him as his sales soared. The driver called his base by mobile phone and a replacement bus was sent, arriving an hour later.

I had booked a trip from Bali to Gili Trawangan, a bus journey of about two hours, followed by a four-hour boat trip. That time scale had now been extended. Travel in this part of the world is often an adventure.

The replacement bus got us to Padangbai, a fishing village and ferry port on Bali, where we boarded a Phinisi Schooner, a traditional wooden-hulled vessel. Four hours later, I was stepping ashore from the small tender that took us from the big boat to the palm-fringed beach of Gili Trawangan, a great favourite with backpackers.

Many come here to learn to dive, or gain experience, in contrast with other places where I had been in the company of experienced divers. On my first day, the dive guide was giving his briefing on board the boat. He finished by saying the dive time would be about 45 minutes. My eyebrows shot up.

"Only forty-five minutes?" I asked.

"If good on air, maybe fifty minutes."

"Or more?"

His eyebrows shot up. "More than fifty minutes, John?"

"I'd be affronted if I couldn't."

"Okay. Maybe one hour?"

"Aye, and a bit more." I like to get value for money.

"Okay. We'll see how we go on air. If the others are low on air and have to go up, I will take them up, and then come back to buddy with you."

All but one of the group were on their way up at forty minutes. The other diver stayed with me while Kandar, our guide, saw the others back on the boat, then re-joined us to continue the dive. The other guy was running low on air after 67 minutes. That was respectable and I agreed to go up, though I still had plenty of air left.

The following morning, Kandar took me aside and suggested an alternative to the planned dive with a group of people. A boatload of divers was headed to the west side of the island, but it could drop us off at the south end, just the two of us, and we could do a nice drift dive parallel to the shore, and finish our dive opposite the dive shop. Kandar could have an easy dive escorting me, letting me take pictures without having to worry about anyone else. It would suit the others too. They would not have to sit on the boat for half an hour, waiting for me to surface. We dropped off first and had an interesting 75-minute dive back to base.

When Kandar reported back to Ben, his boss, eyebrows were raised. "Seventy-five minutes? Geez!" Ben then suggested it would be better if I had Kandar as my personal guide, and we dived away from the others from then on. Our next dive lasted 84 minutes.

Word got around. An English guy asked me, "Is it true you did an 85-minute dive yesterday, John?"

"No. That's an exaggeration."

"Yeah, I thought somebody must have got it wrong."

"Aye, it was only 84 minutes." He nearly choked.

Coming ashore the following day, Ben called out, "How long was it today, John?"

"Eighty-one minutes."

"Oh, just a short one, today?"

"Aye. My guide ran out of air."

Even the room cleaners heard the stories. It had now become a ritual. "How long you dive today, Mr John?" asked Ira, the housekeeper, and beamed at me when I told her.

"Oh, Mr John, you may be old man, but you very strong. Mr Alan, he young man, but only dive 45 minutes. Not good as you!" She giggled and gazed longingly at my manly, strong body.... Okay, okay, I am getting carried away now, just a little.... Maybe.

When I returned the following year, Ben took me aside. "Look John, there is no point in you going with all these other divers. I need to get out of the office and take some pictures, so I'll be your guide while you're here. We'll drop off away from the crowds and do our own thing. I know where we can find some good specimens for photography. I have discovered a superb muck dive site over at Lombok, but I keep quiet about it. It is only for experienced divers, but there are loads of interesting critters living there."

So Ben and I, and Sue Lyn Lim, a Malaysian girl, formed a buddy team and had some long photographic dives. The muck dive at Lombok, under a jetty, stretched to 91 minutes. Chatting to Sue on the way back, she had asked about my travels and remarked, "Hey, you are one cool dude, John."

On our return, we compared photographs. Ben had captured a nice image of what we thought was a baby mimic octopus. I found a photo on my laptop of an adult mimic octopus for comparison, while Ben called over a Frenchman who was allegedly an expert. He looked at Ben's photo and was undecided. I offered my photo of the mature one.

"Ah yes. It is a mimic octopus, Ben," he exclaimed. "Look at the internet photo here and you will see the similar features."

"That's not an internet photo, that's John's photo," said Ben.

"No, that is an internet photo he has downloaded," the Frenchman insisted.

His ignorance and arrogance, expressed in such a dismissive manner, raised my hackles. I was not such a cool dude now.

I growled, "That *is* my photo."

"No… You cannot take a photo of that quality with *that* little camera," he said, dismissing my claim with one of those disdainful, effeminate, sweeping gestures with his hand. "You have downloaded that from the internet!"

Mimic Octopus

We don't go in much for disdainful, effeminate, gestures in the Highlands of Scotland, nor do we take kindly to allegations of dishonesty and, as I was no longer cool, I came very near to slapping his stupid, arrogant, effeminate face. However, with remarkable self-restraint, I growled again at him.

"Listen. That photo *was* taken *wi' that wee camera*! And the computer will show the details of where and when it was taken to prove it to you." I then drew his attention to the date, time, place, camera make and model, etc, all details that the computer stores with every photo taken from the camera. The evidence was overwhelming. His opposition crumbled, like Napoleon's army at the battle of Waterloo.

He backed off, muttering, "Oh. I could not imagine you could have taken a photo like that with *that* little camera."

"Aye, weel ye ken noo," I growled. (*Yes, well you know now*, to phrase it in standard English).

Inwardly, I was smiling. Not just because I'd won the argument and punctured his insufferable, over-inflated ego, but because he had paid me a great compliment, albeit unintentionally. He had been convinced that it was a photograph taken by a professional. And *that* was cool.

Gili Trawangan is only about three miles in circumference, a low island with coconut palms and a hump in the middle. There is no motorised traffic, only bicycles and horse drawn taxis. Life on such islands is very laid-back, and the locals are a happy-go-lucky bunch who take each day as it comes: don't worry, be happy, and everything will be all right.

After dinner on my first night there, I walked along what passes for a roadway round the island; a sandy track, but paved with concrete blocks in the section where most of the dive shops and restaurants are located.

Gili Trawangan taxi

Three young men were sitting by the roadside, strumming guitars, so I took my spoons and asked if I could join them. A couple of minutes later, a bike bearing an Australian woman stopped. She listened for a moment and exclaimed, in cultured Australian tones, "Bloody hell mate, that's brilliant! What's that you're playing?" She told me I should be at the Sama Sama Bar where they have jam sessions every night. Any visitor who can play or sing is invited to join in with the resident band. "I can tell you right now, mate, if you go and play your spoons there, they'll love it. You'll be a Trawangan legend within 24 hours."

The boys I was playing with took me there, and introduced me to the band. "Let's hear you play," said one. I struck up, accompanying the recorded music that was being played during the interval. They all grinned. "Hey, that's cool, man," said the leader, followed by something in Indonesian to my friend who had brought me.

"They want you to play with them," he said.

The Sama Sama Bar was a small, open, rectangular area under a thatched roof, with picnic tables around it. The music the band played was rock and roll, rhythm and blues, and reggae, with Bob Marley songs particularly popular. The boys in the band were great to play with. It comprised a couple of guitars, a bass, and a jimbe (a drum played with the hands), with me adding my tippy-tappy accompaniment to the percussion section. The drummer and I soon established a musical rapport, almost a kind of telepathic communication, enabling us to compliment and inspire each other's percussive contributions, and the guitarists grinned their appreciation. The bassist's face was like the moon; big, round, and chubby. When he liked something I had played well he smiled, and his eyes disappeared into the creases in his big, ball-shaped face, white teeth shining against his dark skin.

They realised the potential of the spoons to enhance some of the tunes. They asked me to do a rasping percussion lead as an intro into Back Magic Woman. It gave it that authentic voodoo rasping sound. In others, they gave me a percussion solo, with a call from the vocalist to "Take it, Mistah John!"

I belted out some lively improvisation, left hand whirling, working wonders with the sounds it created. How it does it, I do not know. If I think about my left hand everything goes to pot; if I let it do its own thing it makes magic. That had the audience clapping and cheering, and at the end of the tune the vocalist called for another round of applause, "For Mistah John – what amazing playing."

It was just as the Australian woman had predicted. The boys in the band loved it, the audience loved it, and the owner of the bar loved it as more people crowded in to hear what was being played. The bar sales soared, and the more they drank, the better we sounded.

The sound of the spoons had carried out across the beach, and three young Germans who heard it came in to satisfy their curiosity. They stayed till the bar closed at 2 a.m. and then collared me to see my instrument, telling me that was what had attracted them. Next day, on my way up the beach from the dive boat after my early morning dive, voices called out, "Hey John, you playing tonight?" The news had spread: some of the dive guides, all local lads, told me they had heard about it from their friends, and they came along to hear me play in the nights that followed. Several of the divers came too. Tourists walking past as I was having lunch (it's all open-air restaurants here), smiled and waved, "Hi John," and flapped their hands, mimicking the playing of spoons. The bar takings increased, and the bar owner expressed his appreciation: "Your drinks are always on the house, John."

And that went on every night for the two weeks I was there. One night, a young Irishman held out his hand in greeting. "That was absolutely bloody brilliant," he exclaimed in his rich southern Irish brogue. "Oi couldn't take me eyes off yer hands. The sounds ya get outa yer spoons, it's chust amazin'! We've come here to watch ya this past three nights. When we arrived, people told us we had to go to the Sama Sama Bar to hear this fantastic reggae band wit' a Scottish guy called John, who plays the spoons. Ye're famous! Everybody on the island is talkin' abou' cha."

One night, a guest band came over from Lombok to play the second half of the evening. Their style of music was slow romantic stuff. I sat with the resident band to listen. An Australian girl approached the stage and confronted the Lombok band.

"Where's John? Get John up there with his spoons!"

When told their style of music was not appropriate for spoons, her face fell and she cried out in cultured Aussie tones, "Aw faaack. I only came here to see John playing his faaacking spoons!"

As I was about to leave after my last performance, the boys in the band thanked me and dedicated their next song to me. *"I'm leaving on a jet plane, don't know when I'll be back again."* The audience clapped and cheered and many shook my hand and wished me well. I have returned to that island five times and each time had the same fantastic reception. On landing the following year, I had barely taken five steps from the boat when one guy approached me, held out his hand and said, "John, you have come back again! Did you bring your spoons?"

The Australian woman on that first night was right. I had become a Trawangan Legend.

Chapter 14

KOMODO DRAGONS

The day did not start well. I had ordered an early breakfast at my hotel in Bali, but the chef forgot my order. After I complained, there wasn't enough time to eat it. By the time it arrived, I had already checked out and my taxi was waiting to take me to the airport. I departed hungry and angry.

Getting to Komodo takes a wee bit of effort, even if you are already in Indonesia. Some live-aboard dive boats depart from Bali and offer a cruise for a day or two before getting to Komodo, or you can fly to Flores, which takes about an hour from Bali – if all goes well. That's always a qualification that should be added when booking flights in Indonesia. This time all did not go well.

On arrival at the check-in desk, I was told my flight to Flores had been cancelled due to a technical fault with the aircraft. My face fell. I had to connect with a live-aboard dive boat. Someone would be waiting at the airport to pick me up and take me to the boat. The boat would have to sail without me. The girl told me she had tried to get me on a flight with another airline, but they hadn't enough room for me. I noticed on her passenger list that my name was at the bottom of the list. I queried this as I had booked the flight four months before. I was more likely to have been their first booking, rather than their last. She had no answer to that. She had just been given the sheet and the unpleasant job of telling the few who were stranded what their fate would be.

I asked her to allow me to use her phone. I called the local agency that had arranged the tickets for me. With some Indonesian airlines it is not possible to book online, so you have to do it through a local agency. Although they'd had my booking four months earlier, they had only informed the airline the day before, which is why I was last on the list. I demanded the attention of the manager. I told him about my dive boat connection and how much this trip had cost me and, if I missed the boat, I would be suing his agency for every penny, plus additional costs for extra hotel stays, discomfort and disappointment, and would spread the story of his company's negligence over every social media outlet. He assured me he would get his staff working on this and asked me to wait there.

I waited, looking as grim as a fundamentalist Presbyterian minister preaching hell-fire and damnation to a sinful congregation on a wet and windswept Sunday in Stornoway – and if you have never been to Stornoway on a wet and windswept Sunday, believe me, it doesn't get much grimmer than that!

Thirty minutes later, the phone rang and I heard my name being mentioned. Another plane had been found for me. After flying over the chain of volcanic islands that stretches eastwards from Java towards Timor, I landed at Labuan Bajo on Flores. A car was waiting there to take me to the dock and I was bounced by fast boat about 20 miles through an archipelago of small islands to the traditional Indonesian schooner, Mona Lisa, lying at anchor in a bay.

I was welcomed aboard by Deirdre, our Irish divemaster, and one of the crew with a tray laden with delicious fruit drinks. This was more like it. I was happy to be afloat on a sturdy, wooden sailing vessel; the food was good, and there was plenty of it. The diving was eagerly anticipated, but so too was a run ashore to catch a glimpse of the world's largest venomous lizard, the Komodo Dragon.

From a mud pool in the otherwise dried-up riverbed, a water buffalo drew copious quantities of muddy water into its mouth with a great sucking sound. Down went the head again and more filthy water entered its mouth until its thirst was slaked. Then it was time to lie down and cool off in the water. It lay there, refreshing itself in the shade of the trees that lined the banks of the creek, a welcome escape from the tyranny of the blistering sun.

Three small pools of spring water were the only wet parts of the entire watercourse. The rest was a dry creek, lined by trees which drew their moisture from deep in the soil, their roots branching out on the surface like the tentacles of an octopus, much the same colour as the soil. These few pools of water were essential for survival for the buffalo, pigs, and deer that inhabit these islands. But while the pools offered life-saving water, they also presented the most serious risk to the lives of the animals that drank there. For motionless among the stone-grey roots of the trees, and difficult to distinguish from them by the textured camouflage of their skin, lay several large lizards up to 3 metres long – the deadly Komodo Dragons.

Statuesque, sinister, opportunist killers, they waited. When the buffalo lay down and relaxed, enjoying the soothing relief of the water on its hot skin, the dreadful moment arrived. A dragon made a sudden lunge down the river bank and plunged its teeth into the rump of the buffalo. One venomous bite was all that was necessary for a slow, but certain, death. The dragon withdrew as the buffalo bellowed in pain and thrashed its hooves, struggling to get to its feet. All the dragons had to do now was wait. It could take a couple of weeks for the buffalo to weaken, before it would lie down in a panting heap. The dragons would stalk it, waiting for that fateful moment, and would then move in for another bite or two to hasten the onset of death. Then the feasting would begin. After gorging themselves on the carcass, they would rest for a month or so, until another opportunist bite would bring another feast day. They eat only about twelve times per year.

It was long thought that it was the saliva of the dragon that injected a lethal cocktail of many types of bacteria into the bloodstream of its prey, causing blood poisoning. However, recent research has revealed that Komodo Dragons have venom glands in their jaws. Within the venom is an anti-coagulant, so the bite continues to bleed. The loss of blood through the wound weakens the prey, and probably allows further infection to enter the blood stream. It also offers a scent which allows the dragons, with keen receptors in their long, forked tongues, to locate and follow their victim till it is ready to drop. We saw two buffaloes that day with the mark of death on them. The one at the pool of water with fresh blood oozing from the bite on its rump, already crawling with flies; and another standing not far off, its head hanging low, gasping in the heat of the mid-day sun. It would soon be dead. It is not a pleasant way to die.

Komodo Dragons

This glimpse of nature in the raw was on Rinca, one of only a handful of islands inhabited by Komodo Dragons. Near the landing stage, a guest-house is provided for those who want to stay overnight. It is built on silts. In the shade underneath, lurked several large dragons attracted by the smell of cooking. This is not a place for the uninitiated to go wandering. It is mandatory to be accompanied by a local guide. As we trekked up the side of the dried-out river, the guide stopped at a bend and whispered, "Look! Eight... no... nine dragons!"

"Where?"

I could see none. Their skin colour and shape blends so well with the soil and tree roots they can be very difficult to spot. And if you present yourself too close to these monsters, well, you may get something worse than a mosquito bite. The nearest monster was a mere five metres in front of me – and I hadn't seen it!

They are at their most active early in the morning after cooling down at night while they sleep. Being cold-blooded, they need to lie in the warmth of the sun for a time. Living for up to fifty years, they survive on a meat diet: deer, pigs, and water buffalo. They bite off large chunks of meat, skin, and bones, and swallow it whole. The digestive enzymes do the rest. When digestion is complete, they regurgitate a solid mass of bone, skin, hoof, and hair formed into a large pellet, in much the same way as an owl will cough up a pellet of the skin and bones of a mouse it has eaten. With a population of around 3000, they are a protected species. Males outnumber females by three to one. The females lay their eggs in burrows, digging several, all but one of which are decoys. She lays the eggs in one, but fills in all of them, and neither predatory animal, nor man, knows which one. She also stands guard over her burrows to protect her eggs.

For protection against the dragons, the guides all carry a stout stick, forked at one end. If a dragon becomes aggressive, they get a poke in the face to fend them off. Although seldom aggressive towards humans, children have been attacked near some of the villages. They are also reputed to have dug up and eaten the corpses of humans from the burial grounds.

The islands here are hilly, savannah grasslands growing on free-draining volcanic ash or sandstone. It is not lush, green grass; more a dull, dead-looking khaki colour. The few trees grow along the edges of the river valleys, which at that time of year were dried-up watercourses waiting for the rainy season.

Our guide was pleased with our trek. We'd spotted 26 dragons, 9 buffalo, and a few eagles soaring overhead on thermal currents. After three hours ashore in the blistering sun, it was a relief to get back aboard Mona Lisa for lunch, with the prospect of an afternoon and evening of diving – and there was no lack of adventure there too.

Chapter 15

DIVING IN THAT?

The diving was not good – it was brilliant. It offered a spectacular variety of marine life, and was outstanding in terms of the colour and dramatic underwater landscapes. And the ferocious Komodo currents offered adventure.

Four experienced divers had been swept away here in an afternoon dive six months before. Their boat couldn't find them before darkness fell and they spent the entire night in the sea, making their way ashore next morning on Rinca, the island I had explored to see the Komodo Dragons. After thirty-six hours of searching, they were spotted on a remote beach by an aircraft.

I was now about to dive the same site from where they had been swept away. A small rocky islet, wedge-shaped, sloping on the north side, with a vertical wall on the south side, it was no more than a barren rock above sea level. Underwater, it was stunning. Covered in soft corals, sponges, anemones, and marine algae, it was a riot of colour. We had timed our dive well, around slack water, that period between the tide changing from the ebb to the flow, but even then the current demanded respect. At one end of the island, Deirdre signalled for us to hang on while she checked the current round the corner. She peered over a rock wall and waved us on. The effects of a current are visible: everything bends to the force of the water, and the fish lie head into it, their tales flapping. Most of the time it had been a moderate drift dive, but the current picked up towards the end.

The change was dramatic. One moment we were gliding along, in still water, the next the entire mass of water was moving, propelling us forward. There was no fighting it: you had to go with the flow. We did, until we reached the end of the islet, where the current swirled round the corner from the opposite direction. The effect of these conflicting currents was a mighty push downwards. Kicking against it had no effect. We were still forced down. Equalising the pressure on the ears, pumping more air into the buoyancy vest, and kicking across the flow, we escaped from this sub-sea waterfall. Hugging the rock face, we managed to claw round the corner into a small, sheltered inlet to complete our 3-minute safety stop before ending the dive.

On breaking the surface, we saw what we had been up against. The surface of the sea, which had been silky-smooth when we went down, had come alive. It was now a fearsome maelstrom: swirling, pock-marked with eddies and whirlpools, sometimes mushrooming upward as contrary currents wrestled with each other. It threw up small waves, fighting and breaking white, as they refused to give way to each other.

When we clambered aboard Mona Lisa from the small boat that had picked us up, some new arrivals looked incredulous: "You were diving in THAT? What have we let ourselves in for?"

We were glad to be out of it. Our timing had been perfect, offering us a memorable dive in serene conditions, but with the sting in the tail to let us know what it could be like. Those currents were evil.

Two sites, Castle Rock and Crystal Rock, were beautiful pinnacles. A dive here late in the afternoon presented an incredible sight. What seemed like millions of fish, of all sizes, shapes, and colours, hovered in a strong current laden with nutrients from deep in the ocean. I slung my reef hook onto a rock, paid out the two metres of line, inflated my vest a little so I had positive buoyancy, and thus anchored, I floated above the rock as though seated on an armchair, and gazed at it all in wonder. It reminded me of the traffic in a busy city centre.

The Cauldron, the name says it all, is a narrow passage between two islands. As the tides ebb and flow, the Pacific Ocean is funnelled and compressed through this slender gap. To complicate matters, the sea bottom rises from deep in the ocean to form a saddle over which the mass of water must flow. and nature has thrown a joker into the pack in the shape of a large hole in the middle of the saddle. The current drops into this giant pothole, deflecting off the bottom and its rocky sides to create a 'washing machine' effect in which currents come at you randomly, from every direction.

And to make life more interesting, on one side there is a deep fissure in the rock wall, with a steep downward slope, pouring more of the Pacific Ocean down on top of you. To swim up this crevice is impossible, but you can claw your way up. When you reach the top, it opens into another circular depression, a smaller 'washing machine,' in which the current will pick you up and hurl you to the surface if you release your grip on the rock. Crawling across this hole, clutching at rocks, you find another crevice leading back down to the main channel. You go shooting down this one with the current and get spat out into the main channel again, by which time it is a case of spread your wings and go with the flow. Like a bird caught in a gale, you fly over the rocky saddle and down into a wide area scattered with large clumps of coral, behind which shoals of fish shelter from the torrent, snapping at the nutrients that come flying past them. You can then hook on to a rock, relax, and enjoy the scene.

That was the gist of the briefing from our divemaster, Deirdre, a sylph-like Irish girl. She followed it by: "You have to be a wee bit crazy to do this dive, but it is fantastic. Do you still want to go?"

I was the only crazy one.

We started the dive mid-way between high and low water when the tide was in maximum flow, and with the gravitational effect of a full moon, it was running faster than normal. We dropped backwards off the small boat that took us to the site, and finned straight for the bottom. There was no time to gather on the surface first: the current would have whipped us away. In her briefing Deirdre had said, "Once you get to the bottom, grab a rock, hold on, and have a look around for a few minutes to watch the fish."

Aye, right… She knew the site well and grabbed what seemed to be the only bit of rock attached to the sea bed. I was left to grasp at rounded boulders the size of watermelons, and every one came loose in my hands. Finning like mad to stem the tide, I was still being inched backwards with nothing firm to hold on to. On reaching a hump, an upwelling hoisted me off the seabed with a boulder still in my hands, ascending feet first, kicking like crazy to stay down.

I dropped my rock to grab for the dump valve in my buoyancy vest and yanked it hard. The air inside bubbled out, and I managed to make it back to the bottom, where once again I could find nothing but rocks that came loose in my hands. Deirdre, realising there was no way I could fight back against the current to where she was, relinquished her perch. We flew like birds through the channel to the cauldron, dropped down into the hole and clutched at the bottom, digging our hands into the sand to act as anchors. But the sand was loose, like sugar. In the constant turbulence it never gets a chance to settle and consolidate. With currents buffeting us from every direction, we were constantly being dragged out and having to re-anchor ourselves. It was not easy diving, but it was fun.

Then came the fissure on the side. The current attacked us with ferocity as we clawed our way up the rocky cleft. Imagine trying to climb up a waterfall and you'll get the idea. On reaching the smaller 'washing machine' at the top, we crabbed sideways, clawed ourselves out and over a reef, to find ourselves in a Garden of Eden, a small bay covered in the most glorious corals, sporting every colour in the spectrum – and not the slightest hint of a current! The contrast was unbelievable. We cruised around this coral garden, gazing in wonder, completing our safety stop before surfacing.

When we had clambered aboard the small boat, we looked at each other.

"Well, what did you think of that?" said Deirdre, grinning.

"I think you are the most selfish, wicked, bitch alive!" I growled. "You went down there and grabbed the only piece of rock attached to the bottom, and sat there laughing at me fighting for my life with all these loose stones and up-currents."

She giggled. "I couldn't help it. It was so funny to see you raking every rock off the bottom and reversing feet first to the surface, but you did the right thing and got down safely. What did you think of the scenery?"

"Scenery? I never got the chance to see scenery! I was too intent on saving my life!"

She laughed again. "Oh well, we'll just have to do it again tomorrow so that you can have a proper look at it. What do you think of that for the first dive in the morning, before breakfast?"

"You're a sadist!"

"Och, I know," she replied in her disarming Irish accent, but the challenge in her smile was irresistible. There was no way I could back off and let this Irish slip-of-a-girl get the better of me. I looked her straight in the eye.

"Do it again? No problem. As often as you like."

"Great!" she grinned. "I just love that dive. First dive tomorrow morning it is then."

This time it was towards the end of the ebb, so the current was just strong enough to make the dive interesting, but not so fiendish as it had been at the peak of the flood tide.

And this time I did see the scenery: a dramatic undersea canyon with sheer sides, awe inspiring and splashed with colour, teeming with fish of all sizes. The day before it had resented our intrusion and was intent on destroying us, but that morning it enchanted us with its beauty and charm, allowing us to explore everything it had to offer.

"I love The Cauldron," said Deirdre, as we sat on the wee boat taking us back to the Mona Lisa, lying at her mooring.

"Me too. That was one of the most memorable dives ever."

After each dive, when we came back aboard Mona Lisa, the crew set out delicious fresh pineapple chunks and slices of watermelon, cool drinks, and light snacks to refresh us until lunch or dinner was served. Dining on deck in the warmth of the tropical night, we watched the moon rise over the islands, its moonbeam a brush stroke of pale gold on the surface of the ocean.

That voyage was worth every penny. A comfortable ship, a good crew, and Deirdre, an excellent divemaster. She briefed us well, and shepherded us around dive sites which rank among the most thrilling in the world. Komodo is challenging, but well worth the effort if your experience is up to it.

At the end of the voyage, we were each presented with a map of the Komodo National Park with our dive sites marked on it. On the back of mine, Deirdre had written a wee note:

Dear John,

It's been a pleasure diving with you throughout this trip! It's been super-relaxing for me to dive with somebody so competent and appreciative of the underwater beauty of Komodo waters. Enjoy the rest of your trip – take care and dive safely.

Deirdre.

She wasn't such a wicked bitch after all.

Chapter 16
BAREFOOT IN BAT SHIT

It doesn't sound attractive, but walking barefoot in bat shit was like parading over a warm carpet. For that is what it was; a carpet of dung, composting away, generating a warmth that cossets your bare feet. It felt as though the cave had underfloor heating.

I was in the Raja Ampat islands. At the eastern extremity of the 18,000 islands that make up the state of Indonesia, and about 30 miles south of the equator, you'll have trouble locating these islands on a map. They are a cluster of small limestone islands about fifty miles north-west of Papua, which lies to the north of Australia. The eastern half of the island, Papua New Guinea, is in the British Commonwealth of Nations. The western part, Irian Jaya, is part of Indonesia.

It is not all that long since cannibalism was practiced on Papua, and perhaps may still be in some mountain valleys where tribes have only become known to the outside world within the past few decades. The interior of this large island is one of the least explored areas on the planet, and I would not rule out the possibility that you might appear on their menu if you were bold enough to venture in there and annoy them.

Taking a break from diving, a jungle trail over Kri, the island I was living on, offered an equatorial rain forest experience: dense foliage, dripping wet in the almost 100% humidity, large colourful butterflies, the occasional snake, lizards, strange birds, mysterious rustlings in the undergrowth. This was a little-used trail: the conclusive evidence came in a disconcerting encounter with a large spider's web. Strung out across the pathway, it was about a metre in diameter, with strands like sticky wire. It's large size hinted that it must be home, and a trap for prey, to a very large spider. It was.

No matter how big the spider, when it is hanging in the middle of its web it blends so well with the dappled shades of the backcloth of jungle. You just don't see it until you can see the whites of its eyes, and that is what makes it disconcerting. To have that strong, sticky web wrapped around your face is an arresting experience. However, the huge, long-legged spider (it's legs would have covered my hand if it sat on it) scuttled up one of the lines suspending the web and hid itself among the foliage, while I tried to tear its web from my face. Like wire dipped in superglue, it was sticky and strong. It gives you a kind of horror-movie feeling to be trapped in a web, but the 'keep cool' side of my brain kicked in, and I took comfort from the thought that I looked even more terrifying to the spider when *it* saw the whites of *my* eyes. After all, I did not look anything like a fly, or any other flying animal that might be on its menu.

After a few days exploring the magnificent reefs near the small island of Kri, Maya, the manager of the Kri Eco Resort, suggested a day-trip to some far-off islands for a conventional reef dive, followed by an adrenalin-surging, underwater rush through 'The Passage.' This narrow limestone gorge between two islands is littered with underwater rocks and caves, and the sea pours through it like a river in full flood. Impressive – some say terrifying – it feels as if you are flying, such is the speed at which you hurtle along in the raging current, dodging huge rocks that emerge out of the gloom. It was more of a breathtaking rollercoaster ride than a serious dive – just a wee bit of fun.

And the fun continued when we went to the bat cave, a large A-shaped black hole in a limestone cliff. The white, fang-like appearance of the stalactites made it look like a gigantic mouth, hung with rows of pointed teeth.

The boat eased its way inside the cavern and came to a halt against a pile of fallen rocks, a roof-fall from a long time back. At the top of this heap of rocks was a dark hole leading to the inner chamber, from which could be heard the squeaking of bats, lots of them. Snakes inhabit this cave too. They slither up the rough walls to feast on the bats. Our dive guide, Bija, asked if anyone wanted to go in. Heads were shaken all round the boat. I couldn't believe it.

"No way am I going in there!" muttered a worried-looking American from New York.

I don't get it. This was a guy who scorned taking any precautions against malaria in one of the areas in the world in which it is endemic, yet he wouldn't go into a cave to see some harmless bats? I think he got his risk assessments all wrong, but "Up to you," as they say in this part of the world.

"Count me in," I said.

"Okay, if you are going, I will go too," said Joost, a Dutchman.

We prepared to step ashore to see what the cave held in store for us. Bija looked at me incredulously.

"Are you not putting on your diving bootees?"

"With ten toes for grip I am less likely to slip than wearing rubber soled shoes."

"But the cave is full of batshit!"

"Aye, that's what I would expect. Let's go." I stepped ashore and climbed up the rocks, followed by Joost. Once over the top of the ridge and into the cavernous chamber, our torch beams revealed an astonishing sight. Hanging from the roof were millions of black bats, their eyes sparkling like diamonds in the light of our torches. It was like looking down on the lights of a city from a plane high in the sky.

Bats droppings are small. On falling to the floor, they are devoured by the thousands of fat beetles that scuttle about and pounce on any fresh dinner that rains down from above. Their digestive systems convert the bat droppings into a carpet of warm, dry, crumbly material very much like the garden compost you buy for your pot plants. That means your feet seldom make contact with fresh bat shit – it's actually beetle shit by the time your feet get to it.

Even more remarkable is the heat this process generates. The composting process makes the carpet glow with warmth, and the radiant heat it exudes then heats up the atmosphere in the cave. It would make a lovely warm bed to lie on, apart from the fact that bat droppings would rain down on you, and hungry beetles would be crawling all over you, in pursuit of their food as you slept. There was a bit of odour, but it was not sickening. You soon get used to it.

The diving in the Raja Ampat islands was exceptional. Until recently, Cape Kri held the record for the highest number of different fish species recorded in one dive (284), documented by an American scientist, but Tanjung Papisol, in Triton Bay, Papua, has broken that record with 330. Add to that the hundreds of different corals and sponges, the multi-coloured algae that clothe the rocks, the awesome limestone caves, canyons, and cathedral-like overhangs festooned with marine growth in every texture and hue, and you have an amazing, undersea world.

Raja Ampat's undersea landscape

Among these hundreds of islands, and even more reefs, the tide surges and swirls, producing strong currents laden with nutrients that attract a diverse range of fish, including the giants of the marine world: whales, sharks, manta rays, sting rays, napoleon wrasse, the odd-looking bumphead parrot fish, turtles, and wobbegong sharks which lie, well camouflaged, on the sea bed and let dinner come within range of their large snapping jaws.

Dense schools of sardines, jacks, snappers, and barracuda hover and circle in their hundreds and thousands, and among the corals the wee fish glow in all the colours of the rainbow. All the small stuff; the pygmy seahorses, pipefish, sea-moths, nudibranchs, and flatworms are there too in this pristine environment.

There are 110 dive sites within a short distance of Kri island, and much more of this territory has yet to be explored. It is not the easiest place in the world to get to, but that is good for the diving, because the trouble and expense of getting there means that the relatively few divers who venture this far are usually experienced enthusiasts.

The resort at Kri is a cluster of traditional Papuan huts constructed of bamboo poles and woven leaves, perched on stilts over the sea. The islands are all steep, limestone rock formations covered in dense rain forest, so it is easier to build over the water. That also has the advantage of taking your sleeping quarters away from the jungle and its mosquitoes. The almost constant, slight breeze over the sea means that there is no need for air-conditioning. Lift the covers over the hole in the wall that serves as a window (no glass required), and the air drifts through and allows you to sleep at a pleasant temperature.

The open-sided restaurant was also built over the water, and served delicious food. The communal toilets on the shore have western style flushing to a sceptic tank. They were open-air style, with a space between the four walls and the roof to allow odours to escape. Showers? You poured a pot of water over your head. Life was simple, but pleasant.

To get there, you need to fly into Sorong on Papua. The resort boat then takes you on bouncy 50-mile ride to Kri. There is little tourism on Papua. With less than a thousand visitors per annum, nearly all divers, pale-faced northerners like me are a rarity and aroused the interest of the Papuans. They often stared, with child-like curiosity. A smile to them, a wave, or a greeting, "Selamat pagi. Apa kabar?"

(Good morning. How are you?) elicited the response, "Baik,"(I'm fine) with a warm smile. Others called out, "How are you mister?" (even if you were a woman!). Sorong, as a town, has little to commend it, but the people I encountered made it a charming experience.

The Papuan girls who worked in the resort as chambermaids, waitresses, and cooks were forever laughing and teasing me, each one telling me conspiratorially that one of the others wanted to marry me. Boya sidled up to me and whispered, "John, you like Rina? She wants to marry you." Then Rina approached me later and whispered, "John, you like Heni? She wants to marry you." Never in my life did I feel so desirable! The resort management encouraged them to learn English and provided books for them to study, and I helped out with some informal lessons when I wasn't diving. I enjoyed it, and so apparently did they. The girls were always crowding around me to practice their English – or so they said.

This intrigued the guys. Bija, my dive guide, collared me on the last night. "Hey John, what's your secret? How come you always get all the girls around you?"

I shrugged. "Dunno. It beats me." I wasn't even wearing my kilt when I was there.

When I appeared in the restaurant for my final lunch before departure, the girls in the kitchen, the waitresses, and several of the male staff were seated around the table and started clapping as I entered. When I arrived at the jetty, the manager and the two assistant managers came to see me off. That was normal; but the girls were all there too, with hugs, joking, and laughter as each one lined up, giggling, for her turn to say goodbye. The guys stood around grinning and winking, giving me the thumbs up sign. As the boat eased away from the jetty they waved and called out, "We never forget you, John. Hope you come back again."

After an overnight stay in Sorong, I took a morning flight to Manado, in North Sulawesi. The aircraft was an elderly, twin-engined, propeller driven thing with limited luggage capacity. The cabin luggage bins were so small even my hand luggage had to go in the hold. I could only take my laptop into the cabin with me. When the flight attendant sat down for take-off, she looked nervously out of the window, prayed, and crossed herself two or three times. That makes you think. She did the same when we were landing, and the engines in reverse thrust sent the most alarming, teeth-rattling vibration throughout the plane. On arrival at Manado, only about half the passengers' luggage was delivered to the carousel. Mine was not among it. The excuse was that the aircraft would have been overweight. The rest would come on the next day's flight.

I rented a set of dive gear at Lembeh, where I planned to spend the next few days, and my luggage did arrive next day. A couple from the UK had connecting flights to Singapore that same day, and then on to London. I wondered when their luggage would catch up with them.

Indonesia is a fascinating country. I found its people welcoming everywhere I went, but the local airlines must rank among the most shambolic in the world. Planes disappear into the jungle from time to time, never to be seen again. Ancient aircraft, with many body-work patches, have worn-out seats salvaged from scrapped aircraft, judging by the number of logos of other world airlines stamped on the backs of the seats. The toilet door on this plane would not close, so I had to stand on one foot to pee into the bowl from afar, with the other foot out behind me holding the door closed. The signs on the wall of the toilet were in Greek.

This country is full of surprises, especially when you are travelling.

Chapter 17

DECEPTIONS

Lembeh Strait, a bustling shipping lane off North Sulawesi, has container ships making for the terminal, and fishing vessels in all shapes and sizes rushing their catch to the fish dock for the early morning market. With such activity, a fair bit of rubbish lies on the bottom: oil drums, bits of rope and netting tangled with isolated coral growths, bits of wreckage, banks of volcanic clinker and black, volcanic, coarse sand. Not quite the diver's dream of colourful corals, anemones and sponges, but Lembeh offers a different kind of experience. It is the muck-diving capital of the world.

As you descend, it looks like a desert with bits of rubbish strewn around. But don't be deceived, for this undersea junkyard is home to an astonishing variety of odd-looking animals that find it easy to burrow or wriggle themselves into the loose sand, soft mud, or under heaps of rubbish, where they await the arrival of their unsuspecting prey.

The aptly named stargazer, a sluggish looking, fat-bodied fish, lies hidden in the sand, except for its two eyes looking up to the sky. Its mouth faces upwards too, waiting for a snack. The two eyes resemble pebbles on the bottom; a clever deception. A small fish swims past, and with amazing rapidity the stargazer's jaw opens and snaps shut. Sluggish? Not when food swims past.

Stargazer

Not far away, what looks like a stone on the bottom is a large snake eel, whose head appears like a small dark cone with only eyes, nose and mouth showing, the rest of its long body hidden in the sand. Weird-looking devilfish have pectoral fins they use as legs for walking along the bottom. Looking like an old piece of wreckage is their disguise, and despite their cumbersome plodding there is nothing slow about the speed with which those jaws open and close, faster than the eye can take in. Everything here seems deceptive.

The flying gurnard is another that seems to prefer walking to swimming. When surrounded by strange beings like divers, they spread elongated fins that look like a fan and run around on the bottom, rather than use the fins for swimming to escape. When their large pectoral fins open fully, the markings resemble a large cat's face, presenting a startling defensive mimicry to deceive its pursuer.

The mimic octopus, a small slim-line version of the octopus, is capable of mimicking several other sea creatures. It will slither along the bottom and eases its flexible body, and all those eight tentacles, into the sand to disappear underground like magic. The wunderpus is similar. Cuttlefish and squid also inhabit this place. The tiny blue-ringed octopus is a magnet for photographers. Small enough to fit into the palm of your hand, and cute in appearance, they flash blue rings on their skin when threatened. This makes them look pretty, but that warning is serious. Their bite is deadly. An Australian is reported to have picked one up and brought it out of the water for his family to see. It wriggled up his arm and bit him on the neck. Limb by limb, organ by organ, his entire body became paralysed and shut itself down. He was conscious the whole time until, last of all, his brain closed down. It took about 90 minutes for the bite from that one tiny animal to take him through the nightmare awareness of total paralysis to end his life. The golden rule is: look, but don't touch.

Blue-ringed Octopus

It only takes 1.5 milligrams of sea snake venom to kill a man. One bite from a sea snake will inject 15 milligrams of venom into your blood stream, enough to kill you ten times over. This was one of the interesting facts I read in a book on the marine life of Indonesia. Sea snakes are not often aggressive. Fatalities from bites tend to be fishermen untangling the odd sea snake that gets caught up in their nets. Unconcerned about divers, they will often come close as they pass, intent on their own business. However, the book I was reading went to some length to amend the view that sea snakes are *never* aggressive, describing how one repeatedly attacked and tried to bite a floating oil drum as it was being hauled to the boat from the shore: so much for the docile reputation. The message is clear. Never take things for granted. And keep your hands to yourself.

All this flashed through my mind two days later, when I came face to face with a sea snake. Towards the end of the dive, I spotted it exploring the coral underneath me. Taking photos, I followed it as it wound its way among the corals. Eager to get a good picture of its face, I hovered about a metre above an opening where I expected it would reappear. My patience was rewarded. It emerged, looked up, and made straight for me. The passage in that book came into mind. This one had a determined gleam in its eye as it shot up to face me.

An animal may become aggressive if it feels threatened, and strike out at you. I had been hovering above it, like the paparazzi that follow the rich and famous to intrude upon their privacy to sneak an intimate photo. Escape was out of the question as I could never move faster than it could. I could only sit and wait for whatever fate had in store for me. It pushed its face right against the camera lens, turning its head slightly to look inside the lens. It paused there, poking at the lens with its nose, as if trying to get inside this dark hole that was in front of it. I had wanted a picture of a sea snake, close-up, but not that close! Not within a few millimetres of my delicate, soft skin.

Any movement might trigger alarm in the snake, perhaps causing it to bite me. This was not a time for panic. I daren't move until it had satisfied its curiosity. With a rapid flick it was off, making for the surface to breathe. I too flicked round and managed to get another picture of its full length, snaking ahead of me as I followed it to the surface. It was a great way to end the dive.

It is not all mud and muck at Lembeh. Towards the western entrance to the strait, large Gorgonian fans offer a habitat for pygmy seahorses. Highly sought-after, but challenging subjects for photographers, they are extremely difficult to detect, but the dive guides know their patch and can always find them for you.

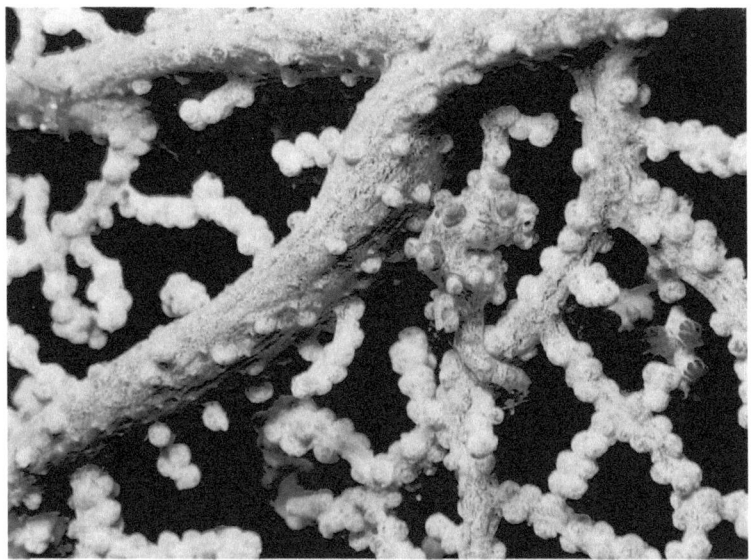

Pygmy seahorse blending with its background

Being small is part of their defence. Only about 2cms, (three quarters of an inch) from nose to tail, when the tail curls round the coral to anchor them in position, there is only about half their length left to see, and they blend so well with the corals. Camera shy, they turn away, making it difficult to get shots of their faces. Once in a while you get a good profile shot, and that makes you glow with satisfaction. As with other seahorses, the female deposits her eggs in the male's pouch. He then fertilises them, and carries them through the gestation period of about two weeks, till they hatch. One male has been observed giving birth to 34 babies.

The electric clam is another dazzling performer. Secreting itself in crevices in caves or under overhangs, it's flesh is bright red, with hair-like fronds over the membrane between the two shells. When you approach, it starts flashing what looks like blue streaks of lighting from one end of the membrane to the other. But the lightning is not electric. It was believed for a long time to be a form of bioluminescence, but a research paper published in 2015 explained that it is caused by reflective silica plates, located along its lips, reflecting ambient light. Why they do this is still not clear. It may be that they detect changes in the light as a potential predator approaches and this triggers the lightning effect. It is an effective deterrent. Some divers have wondered if they would get a shock from it.

Electric clam

Each night at dusk, mandarin fish become active and emerge from their hiding places among the coral rubble that lies close to the shore, in about six metres of water. They are small, about the size of your little finger. Coloured in dark green and orange colours, they are difficult to spot in the gloom as night begins to fall. Then the excitement begins. The males come out looking for a female with whom to go roaming in the gloaming. As with humans, the twilight hours seem to evoke a desire for romance, a time for courtship.

The mandarin fish pair up, aligning themselves side-by-side in a vertical position. The male and female then wrap themselves around each other in the most tender, loving embrace. Together they spiral upwards, as if soaring to the heavens in an ecstasy of passion. This only lasts for a few moments, but is beautiful to watch. It would be a hard-hearted observer who would not have his emotions stirred by such a display of tenderness.

We were voyeurs, trying to capture these two tiny fish making such tender and passionate love on camera. Unfortunately, I had mixed up my batteries and placed the ones I had used in the earlier dive back in the camera, instead of the fresh batteries. I had to keep the camera switched off until I saw a union likely to happen, then switch on and try to get the event in focus, but by the time I had done that the moment had passed and the lovers had split and dived back among the coral.

Kungkungan Bay Resort was excellent: great service, good food, comfy rooms, and the waitresses sweet and ever smiling. Richard, one of my dive buddies, a 67 year-old diver from Las Vegas, Nevada, had been there 7 times. He enjoys a glass of Scotch whisky, and told me at dinner one night that he had a bottle of Johnnie Walker stashed away in his room, and he would like me to share a glass with him on my last night there. He chose a table out on the verandah, and explained that if you bring your own drink, they levy a corkage charge. But having been there so often, he had charmed the waitresses, and they smuggled the bottle under the counter and delivered a dram to us out on the verandah for us to enjoy.

Conversation ranged over many topics, one of which happened to be the waitresses. As they served customers at the far end of the verandah, they had to pass our table. You could not be human if your eye was not drawn to them. They were clothed in tight-fitting traditional silk dresses from the neck to the ankle, but with a slit on the left from ankle to mid-thigh.

As each of them passed to serve the other tables, I received a smile, and he got the rear view. I grinned as the conversation faltered while his eyes flicked towards the retreating girl's rear end. When he looked back at me, with a twinkle in his eye, he muttered, "That's the most darned, neat, little ass. It reminds me of two jack rabbits in a sack."

In order to get maximum benefit from a visit to North Sulawesi, a diver ought to consider spending a few days at both Lembeh and Bunaken National Park. Lembeh is a muck diving destination, while Bunaken offers reef diving around the volcanic islands that lie close to Manado.

My final day was spent touring the Minahasa Highlands in North Sulawesi, to get some images of traditional life in this part of

Indonesia. The resort offered a tour, but it was not economical for only one person. Merri, one of the receptionists, suggested it would be much cheaper for me to hire a car and driver, and she volunteered to give up her day off to act as my guide and interpreter. Bright, intelligent, and very knowledgeable about local customs, she was an excellent companion, and I had a great day out with her.

The culture and religion in this northern peninsula of Sulawesi is distinct from that of Java, Sumatra, and Bali. While Indonesia is predominantly Moslem, Bali has a high proportion of Hindus, and in North Sulawesi the majority are Christian. Spices were what attracted the Dutch here. They have a bewildering array of spices for cooking and health, and they use certain spices for embalming, to prevent a corpse from decaying in the steamy tropical heat. Those who owned the clove plantations were the wealthiest in the district.

Dog for dinner

A visit to a traditional market provided shocking images. A cage held some medium-sized dogs, but they were not for sale as pets. They were waiting to be killed, the hair removed by singeing, and then they are laid out on a slab and butchered for human consumption. Also on display were wild pigs, bats, and a kind of white-tailed rat from the rice fields, all waiting for some hungry buyer. Butchering was primitive. The carcasses were chopped up on large blocks of wood saturated with the blood of animals. They were crawling with flies. Blood flowed along porcelain-tiled worktops and dripped to the floors, forming puddles. Beside the dog stall, dog tails and the bottom parts of legs, with the paws, were tossed aside, strewn on the ground beside the stall. The flies had a feast every day. The rats took care of the rest at night. It was perhaps the most nauseating sight and smell I have encountered in all my travels.

We eat sheep, pigs, and cattle, but baulk at eating dogs. Yet the dog is eaten in several countries. We eat birds, so why not bats, rats, and cockroaches, all potential sources of protein. As Merri explained, "In Indonesia we eat everything: Scooby Doo, Mickey Mouse, and Batman."

Chapter 18
AFTER THE TSUNAMI

A 2,300 ton ocean-going barge sits on dry land in the middle of a city, 5 km inland from the sea. Nearby, a fishing boat rests on the roof of an empty shell of a house. It is impossible for the mind to grasp the enormity of what happened in Banda Aceh, at the northern tip of Sumatra, on the morning of Dec 26, 2004.

Barge 5km inland

Stirred up by a massive earthquake measuring 9.1 on the Richter scale, an enormous tidal wave surged in from the sea and devastated the city, sweeping away thousands of dwellings and the people who lived in them to a horrific death. No one knows exactly how many people died that day along the coasts of Sumatra and Thailand. The death toll is in the hundreds of thousands.

Few places in the world are so well placed for destruction by a tsunami. Viewing the city from the air showed just how flat and waterlogged the area is. Scarcely above sea level, a series of huge tidal waves, penetrated far inland, crushing houses, shops, and people, tossing cars around like toys. There was little hope of survival in the face of such a powerful onslaught.

That huge barge, sitting 5 km from the sea, remains a monument to the awesome power of the sea on that day of death. It is only in a few spots like this, where the barge has been left, that there is any evidence of that awful disaster. It remains as a monument to the people who lost their lives, and to the massive international support that the world gave in their time of need, something that the people of that city have not forgotten.

So what do you do with a 2,500 ton barge sitting in the middle of a city far from the sea? Convert it to a power station, and make it an asset! I liked that. Rather than waste energy breaking it up for scrap, they have utilised it as a force for good and, by its sheer incongruity, it serves as a dramatic reminder of what happened there.

A small museum to the tsunami stands a short distance from the barge and the fishing boat on the roof. Its collection of photographs reveals the scale of the devastation and death. Nothing is left out. Shocking photographs of torn bodies piled among the flotsam of broken houses brought home just how these people suffered. It would be too easy to forget when you see how the city has recovered, and it brings home the colossal challenge faced by the relief agencies in bringing food, medical supplies, clothing, and all the essentials of life to a city of hundreds of thousands who had lost everything.

In a park in the city centre stands another monument: a veteran aircraft, a Douglas DC3, often called the Dakota. These aircraft provided sterling service as transport planes during World War II. In 1948, when the Russians blockaded the city of Berlin by refusing to let supplies through by road or canal, the Dakotas flew in supplies, hundreds of them every day, landing and taking off from Templehof Airport every minute or so. The Dakota became a symbol of relief in different parts of the world, bringing aid to those in need, and one now sits on a plinth in Banda Aceh, a testimonial to the flights bringing aid to the devastated city. That particular memorial held some personal significance: age does not necessarily mean decrepitude. These veteran aircraft, with a maximum speed of only around 350 miles an hour, were still offering sterling service 75 years after the first one flew.

Banda Aceh is again a bustling city. But that barge isn't going anywhere. It will remain the most startling reminder of the awesome power of the sea, and a monument to the hundreds of thousands who died in the most awful natural disaster in recorded history.

"Pulau Weh? Where is that?" was the usual response when I mentioned I was going there. A small island just off the northern tip of Sumatra, few people had ever heard of it, even among the diving fraternity. But Roger Talbot, who had been my guide on my second trip to Myanmar had, and he was keen to accompany me to try it out.

After an overnight stay in Banda Aceh, a fast ferry whisked us over to the island in an hour, and a taxi transported us to the Lumba Lumba Dive Centre. On the way, the road was swarming with a clan of monkeys: cute babies playing with each other, tolerant parents and elders strolling down the highway unconcerned about the traffic. Like an extended family out for the day, they all seemed to be enjoying themselves.

The Lumba Lumba Dive Centre snuggled against a steep, tree-covered hill with a sweep of sandy bay before it. It looked idyllic. It was hard to believe that it too had been trashed when the tsunami struck. However, as most of it is located on a steep slope, it had been possible for everyone to escape. Now rebuilt, it is a very pleasant cluster of comfortable bungalows and a dive centre.

Catering was provided by a few small restaurants strung out along the beach. The cooking was done on small gas stoves, which meant it could take some time from ordering until the food was on the table.

They didn't keep much food in stock, and certain dishes had to be ordered the day before to allow them to get the food in. The choice was limited, even more so as they often ran out of things.

I ordered toast and honey at breakfast. Back came the waiter.

"No honey." I had toast without honey.

The next customer ordered toast too. Back came the waiter.

"No toast. Bread finished."

But Mama Doughnut, an elderly lady, brought along a box of freshly cooked doughnuts with various fillings at the end of each day's diving. They were irresistible.

It was a quiet place until nightfall, which was heralded by the sounds of the jungle: the incessant din of cicadas, the croaking of frogs, the flutter of bats, and all the other rustling sounds of the night. Oddly enough, there was the occasional "Moo" as well. A few cattle wandered along the beach each night, and grazed the resort grounds. Goats pranced about as well, browsing among the foliage.

The diving was superb. On the edge of the Indian Ocean, strong, deep-water currents bring lots of nutrients, resulting in a wide variety of fish and several nudibranchs I had never seen before. In stark contrast to the previous two weeks of muck diving, where the emphasis was on finding critters in the mud and sand and among the rubbish, here was underwater spectacle on a grand scale. This is right on the edge of the fault where two tectonic plates of the earth's surface push against each other. The Indian Ocean plate is thrusting itself under the Sumatra coastline, which is why there are so many earthquakes in this region. As the ground is forced upwards it breaks, presenting a rugged underwater landscape covered in colourful marine algae, anemones, sponges, corals, and offering shelter and food for many species of fish.

Dives started deep at around thirty metres, and ended up close to the rocky shore, with a considerable surge from the big Indian Ocean swells that sweep into the bay. You swing back and forth in the surge among those big rocks as though dangling on a pendulum. Large schools of fish seemed to enjoy swinging back and forth too. Powder blue surgeonfish are usually seen in ones and twos, but there were hundreds of them, swinging in the surge among the boulders.

A school of small, striped fish were having a mass egg-laying session among the rocks. The eggs were being spewed out in swarms, and as quick as the eggs were laid, the surgeonfish were swooping in and eating them.

Among the divers were some airline pilots, flying Boeing 767s with Thomson Air who were operating on charter to Garuda, the Indonesian flag carrier. At that time of year, thousands of Moslems fly from Indonesia to Jeddah to make the Hajj, their pilgrimage to Mecca. Extra planes are flown in to cope with the demand, and these pilots were using their off-duty time to enjoy some top class diving. Thousands of Indonesians want to make this pilgrimage before they die, and many are on the brink of death before they set off. Each year around 200 deaths occur on these pilgrimages, so they carry plenty of coffins!

Also diving with us were Jeannie, Janice, and Caviner, three young Singapore teachers starting out on their careers. They had learned that Roger's birthday was coming up, with mine three days later, and they commissioned one of the restaurants to bake a birthday cake for us, keeping it a secret until the night before our departure. After the diving, they insisted we join them for a farewell drink, and the cake was presented for our joint birthday party, another of the unexpected memories of Indonesia.

Chapter 19

ON TOP OF THE WORLD

Borneo is home to the oldest tropical rainforest in the world. Estimated to be 130 million years old, it is 70 million years older than the Amazon rainforest. However, in the last few decades, much of that rainforest has been logged to supply the Malaysian plywood industry, and the natural forest has been replaced with palm oil plantations. These bring economic benefits, but at the loss of a vast natural resource. Commercial exploitation has destroyed a range of plants of importance for their medicinal properties, and so much of the natural habitat of orangutans that they are now an endangered species. That jungle was also home to vast numbers of monkeys, snakes, insects, birds, beetles as big as your hand.

Kota Kinabalu, known generally as KK, is the capital of the province of Sabah in the north of Borneo. It is part of Malaysia along with its southern neighbour, Sarawak. Surrounded completely by Sarawak, is the tiny, oil-rich Sultanate of Brunei, the fifth richest nation in the world. These three lie along the west and north coasts of Borneo in a relatively narrow strip. The rest of Borneo, called Kalimantan, is part of Indonesia.

On my first visit to Borneo, I joined a group of ten travellers on an adventure tour organised by Intrepid Travel, an Australian company. They were all between 20 and 30 years old, apart from one 'oldie', aged 40. At 65 years young at that time, I was the grandfather of the group. A two-hour journey by road and rough mountain track in a four-wheel drive truck took us from modern KK to Kiau Nulu, a mountain village of 70 families. That doesn't sound a lot, but it represents a population of about 700! Women may give birth to as many as twelve, fourteen, and in one case sixteen children. A 50 year-old woman told me she had married at the age of fourteen, became a mother at fifteen, and had fourteen children before her 43rd birthday. Older children help the mother in caring for the younger children with the preparation of food, and the never-ending task of washing the family's clothes. Every house was festooned with garments drying in the sun. The boys help the father on the family land, planting and harvesting fruit and vegetables. Members of the Dusun tribe, they have their own language. We slept in a small bunkhouse owned by the Catholic Church. Christianity only arrived here in the 1960s.

Following a welcome by the headman of the village, a dance troupe from the primary school performed traditional dances to the sound of music played on gongs. They then invited us to try. As each gong has to be struck with a different number of beats from all the others, our efforts resulted in not so much music, more a breach of the peace. However, I decided to play the same game and invited the villagers to try to play the spoons after I had joined them in one tune. They were quite perplexed when they discovered that what looked so easy in my hands defied their best efforts, and it was our turn to laugh.

The ladies of the village prepared our food. We dined sitting cross-legged on the floor. Chairs and tables don't feature in their lives. Dinner consisted of a bowl of rice accompanied by various other dishes concocted from chicken, vegetables, and mountain herbs. After dinner, some of the men of the village arrived with homemade rice wine. They celebrate the Sabbath by drinking rice wine after the church services are over, an interesting idea. Protocol dictated that you had to drink a cup of the stuff without stopping and not leave a drop, demonstrated by turning the cup upside down over your head. If even one drop fell out, you had to drink another cup. It wasn't the best tasting wine I have drunk, so I made sure one cup was enough for me. After that, we were asked to introduce ourselves. Then the music started.

The headman, having seen me play that afternoon, had told me to bring my spoons. All the local lads wanted to try to play, but were no more successful than the others had been earlier. That earned me some respect. All mountain guides or porters, I met several of them a couple of days later on my ascent of Mount Kinabalu, when they greeted me with their hands imitating the playing of the spoons. Mount Kinabalu has brought significant employment to the people who live in its foothills. It has become a magnet for trekkers from all over the world, and this tough form of tourism is bringing significant economic benefits.

Our ascent of Mount Kinabalu was planned in stages to become accustomed to the altitude, thus reducing the risk of altitude sickness. The following night we spent at an altitude of about 6000 feet, where the mountain could now be seen rearing its massive, rocky head high above the ridges clothed in jungle that stretched as far as the eye could see. This was a good place for a warm-up, trekking some of the jungle trails, before tackling the final ascent of the mountain. There's not much fear of getting lost. It is almost impossible to wander off the trail with the vegetation being so dense and the mountain slopes so steep.

Mount Kinabalu

Next morning, we got kitted up for the two-day climb to the summit. Our packs contained changes of clothing and footwear, rainproof gear, toiletries and towel, toilet paper, insect repellent, first-aid kit, two hats (one for shade from the tropical heat, the other for protection against the cold on the high slopes), gloves, and wind-proof jackets for the night climb, and at the summit, sunglasses, cameras, high energy food for snacking, and water; plenty of water.

The plan was to climb to a bunkhouse at 11,000 feet and sleep there. Breakfast was to be at 2 a.m. to be ready to depart at 3 a.m. for the final push to the summit in darkness. The aim was to arrive at the summit at 4,095 metres (13,435 feet) as dawn was breaking. Dawn is the best time of day to be there. Usually the night sky at the summit is clear, with clear mornings. In early morning you see it at its best. As the sun gets higher, it becomes very hot with the risk of heatstroke and severe sunburn. Clouds tend to build up in the afternoons, and that can mean torrential rain, with thunder and lightning. It is wise to get off the baking rocks of the summit plateau before the heat melts the soles of your boots, and find relief in the shade of the forest as you descend. If you are lucky, you might get back dry. Well, no, that's not quite accurate. You may escape before the rain comes, but you will sweat buckets, and your clothing will be drenched anyway.

I declined the offer of a porter to carry my backpack. This mountain is high – and it's uphill all the way – so our guide recommended hiring a porter to carry our packs. For me, it was a matter of self-respect, or just being thrawn (for non-Scottish readers, thrawn means stubborn, but with added attitude). I intended to carry everything myself. My room-mate, an Australian in his late twenties, thought likewise. The others hired porters and travelled light. About a third of those who attempt this climb fail to reach the summit, and looks from some of the group seemed to say, "He'll never make it." But I had other thoughts. Only three young guys in their early twenties reached the top before me, by a mere ten minutes, and they had porters carrying their baggage. The rest of the group was a long way behind. Being thrawn can be so satisfying.

On the way up, it wasn't long before the group began to spread out. The trail is well maintained, and it's virtually impossible to get lost. The guide allowed some of us to go on ahead at out own pace while he stayed with the main (slow) group. The three young guys, unencumbered by any baggage, galloped off ahead. I plodded along at a steady pace to Laban Rata, where the bunkhouse was located.

We climbed into our bunks early to catch some sleep, and after a light breakfast at 2 a.m., we set off, head-torches lighting the way ahead. An agonising start saw us climb up some steep slopes to the end of the tree line. It was all bare rock from there to the summit; a landscape devoid of vegetation, apart for a few hardy alpine plants clinging to crevices between slabs of rock. The rock was very steep and smooth in places and a strong white rope was anchored into the rock, all the way to the summit. On the steep sections, it offered an aide to climbing them; on the more gentle slopes of the summit plateau, its white line was a marker to guide you to Low's Peak, the highest of Kinabalu's several summits. The last few hundred feet were the roughest and most demanding. At that altitude, the air was pretty thin and muscles were begging for more oxygen.

Dawn was not far from breaking as I reached the peak, with just enough light to reveal the nature of the landscape around us. On the way up, it had been a moonless night, sparkling with stars, but my head was focused on the light beam from the head-torch, showing me where to tread on the rough ground. Only dark shadows appeared from time to time to indicate the presence of large rocky outcrops along the way: everything else was obscured by darkness. Now, features of the landscape were being released from the dark shrouds of night, and what was revealed was breathtaking.

Before the sun had appeared above the horizon, a greyish light allowed us a glimpse of steep precipices, dropping down a thousand feet or more. Around us was a panorama of grotesque peaks, a landscape sculpted by nature in her most surreal mood. It was like being on another planet. But when the sun rose above the horizon, these surrounding peaks glowed red, like embers on a fire, a wonderful, warming sight. More and more features were revealed as the sun rose, warming our chilled bodies. It was well worth getting out of bed at 2 a m. to see this.

The warmth of the rising sun and the amazing scene around us dispelled tiredness, and it was with some reluctance that we started our descent down to the National Park HQ over 7000 feet below. That descent put some stress on the knees and thigh muscles, but my trekking poles helped to take the strain.

A short journey by road took us to Poring Hot Springs, the perfect place to end a strenuous day. The springs were hot, but what a relief to my aching legs! I lay back, embraced by their soothing waters, and reflected. Climbing through the steamy heat of the jungle and the chill of the rocky upper slopes, I had reached the top at 13,435 feet, carrying my own pack, and had outperformed most of the youngsters 40 or more years younger than me.

I didn't feel good.

I felt on top of the world.

Chapter 20

BLOODSUCKERS

An interminable bus ride of about 200 miles took us from the mountainous interior around Mt Kinabalu, over the north-eastern lowlands, to the banks of the Kinabatangan River. The magnitude of the jungle clearance that has taken place here is staggering, the rainforest having been cleared and replaced with palm-oil trees, millions of them, planted in straight rows. For at least four of the five hours of the journey, all you could see was palm-oil trees, row after row, mile after boring mile, in a never-changing scene amounting to thousands of square miles of monoculture.

I wonder about the long-term effects of only one kind of tree growing over such a large area. The risk of disease striking the trees could have a devastating effect, laying waste to such a large area, devastating the economy. So much here depends on palm-oil production; planting, harvesting, transporting, processing, sales, marketing, exports. The people employed in it need homes, transport, food, so a lot depends on these palm trees remaining healthy. But as always, the real wealth goes to the foreign investors who drive the commerce forward.

It was with a sense of relief that we entered a conserved area of rainforest. Staying in a village on the banks of the river offered an opportunity to savour some local culture. The villagers welcomed us into their homes and fed us, sitting cross-legged on the floor, eating traditional food with fingers. No forks, knives, or spoons are used, except for serving the food. A bowl of water is offered to wash the hands. They eat with only the right hand, never the left, which traditionally was used for cleaning one's private parts.

I needed two hands, regardless of how I cleaned my private parts. Try eating rice and curry with only your right hand, while sitting on the floor. You are not allowed to have your legs pointing out in front of you as that is regarded as offensive body language; they must be crossed or tucked in behind you. For those unaccustomed to sitting like this, it can be very uncomfortable after a short time. My attempts at eating with my fingers had rice dribbling down my chin and scattering over the rug. I muttered an apology and spat out more rice on the rug. They laughed. The correct technique is to scoop together a portion of rice, compact it with your fingers, gather it up, and flick it into your mouth with your thumb. Easy. Go on. Try it.

They didn't speak much English, understanding only the occasional word. But with a bit of sign language and appropriate body language, we sustained some convoluted conversations. Like the mountain people we had visited a few days earlier, the river people had their own distinct language and spoke that at home, as well as the national language, Bahasa Melayu, or Malay.

My bed was comfortable. The bathroom was a concrete floor with a drain hole at one corner, a barrel of rainwater, and a scoop to pour the cold water over your head. For body waste disposal, you squat over a hole in the floor, with a long drop to a barrel situated beneath the house which was on stilts. A bucket of rainwater and a scoop is used for cleaning private parts afterwards. It's okay after you set your mind to it.

The orangutans and monkeys hide away from the heat of the sun in the middle of the day, so the best time to see them feeding and socialising is in the morning. We rose at 5:30 a.m. for a boat trip up the river, as the jungle is so dense. We spotted three orangutans. A mother, with a baby clinging to her, swung casually from branch to branch about fifty feet up in the canopy. Several varieties of monkey fussed about in noisy gatherings. The proboscis monkeys with their long, drooping noses, are called 'English Monkeys' on account of the English settlers having much bigger noses than the almost flat noses of the indigenous population. Statuesque egrets posed along the river banks, and hornbills with their grotesque beaks fluttered among the high branches.

After breakfast, a villager taught us how to fish using traditional traps made of rattan and bamboo, hung with a bell shaped net: it took some practice to master the technique for casting it on the water and drawing the catch in. A cooking lesson in the community centre came next. Sitting on the floor, we chopped up meat, vegetables, herbs and spices, and cooked them in a wok. I swapped some recipes with the girls who taught us. They know how to make Scottish Shortbread now. The food we cooked was eaten for lunch, after which they put on a display of dancing, wearing colourful traditional costumes, and, as usual, they invited us to join in.

The original plan to go trekking and camping in the jungle was cancelled. Heavy rain the previous week had risen the river level about ten feet higher than normal and a large area, where we intended to camp, was still underwater. In flood conditions, the crocodiles move out of the strong river current and into the still waters of the flooded areas, looking for food and dry banks to rest on, so it was not safe to go wandering through muddy waters for fear of encountering hungry crocodiles about twenty feet in length.

An hour-long trip in a fast, bumpy boat from Sandakan to a tiny island, Pulau Selingaan, provided the most uncomfortable voyage I have ever endured. Going flat out, the boatman sat comfortably in his hydraulically dampened chair, ignoring the discomfort the passengers had to endure sitting on a hard seat. In a steep choppy sea, every wave resulted in a bone-crushing crash with such force that my vertebrae were rattling like castanets, and my brain was thumping against my skull. I wanted to kill him.

On Pulau Selingaan, the turtles come ashore at night to lay their eggs in holes they dig in the sand. The beaches are cleared each day at 6 p.m. to give the turtles priority. At about 9 p.m. we received a call from the beach rangers informing us that we could now view a mother laying her eggs. A big turtle, she laid 82 eggs, all of which were collected in a bucket as there was a turtle conservation project in operation there. The eggs, collected by the ranger as the mother lays them, are placed in holes dug in a hatchery to protect them from predators. Each hole is marked with a stick, with the date and the number of eggs.

Two months later when the babies hatch, the sand erupts, and hordes of tiny turtles emerge to run down the beach for a swim. But with plenty of predatory birds awaiting this migration, those contained in the hatchery are collected, taken to the beach in a box, and released close to the water's edge. They run into the water. A wave comes in and they get swept back again. But they are determined wee things, and plunge back into the sea again and again, until they disappear from view. Most will get eaten: only a small percentage attain maturity. Seeing these cute wee things making their dash for the sea, running along on their flippers, with heads held high, is one of nature's most endearing sights.

Orangutans' breakfast time

Not far from Sandakan is the Orangutan Rehabilitation Centre at Sepilok, where injured or orphaned orangutans are cared for. They are released into the jungle when they are able to fend for themselves. Twice each day, bananas and young bamboo shoots are laid out on a feeding platform in the jungle, with ropes leading to it attached to some distant trees. An empty oil drum is banged at 10 a.m. and 3 p.m. and the orangutans swing in along the ropes from the jungle to have their meal. You can only marvel at their agility and effortless movements – and their facial expressions are so cute. Some cheeky macaque monkeys came in to scavenge the left-overs after the orangutans had had their fill, squabbling and fighting, as monkeys do.

In the afternoon, we had the opportunity to explore the jungle. To my astonishment, only Paul, my Australian room-mate, and I were interested. The others, youngsters in their early twenties, preferred to take a taxi to the town to go to a cinema, instead of plodding through the mud in the dripping, steamy jungle, seeing armies of enormous black ants on the march, hearing monkeys screeching and crashing among the trees high above, listening to strange rustlings, seeing snakes slither into the undergrowth, clawing sticky spiders' webs from your face, and finding yourself on the menu for hordes of bloodthirsty leeches. How could watching a film be better than that?

The heavy rain of the previous couple of days had left the jungle sweating, every leaf dripping with moisture. The trails, such as they were, were mostly ankle deep in mud and rotting leaves. In conditions like these there is no evaporation of the sweat on your body. You can almost imagine green mould growing on your skin. And these are the conditions beloved by leeches.

It wasn't long before regiments of the damned things were swarming from the carpet of leaves, mud, and puddles of the jungle floor, up our legs in a peculiar flicking motion, with head and tail alternating in sticking persistently to skin until they found the right spot. Soft, smooth skin was preferred to the scrub-like hair on my legs. They dropped off leaves on to arms and clothing. With almost every step, the black marauders jumped aboard. I used the back of my thumbnail in a flicking movement to get them off, but they often flicked their tails over and stuck fast again, just as the head was released.

They anaesthetise your skin, so you don't feel them, neither when they climb up your leg, nor when they suck your precious blood. Injecting an anticoagulant into the blood makes it easier for them to suck it out of you. When they climb on, they are as thin as fine string, but after sucking your blood they swell up and drop off, by which time they can be as thick as your thumb. However, after they've had their fill, your blood continues to flow from the wound, and there is a risk of infection getting in. I thought I was doing fine keeping myself clear of them until, near the end of our trek, I felt something inside my sock on my right ankle. I stretched the sock and there was a leech as big as my thumb. It had dined well on me.

Paul, my companion, found one under his shirt, feeding on his stomach just above his belt. I checked in that area too, and as I lifted my shirt, which I had been wearing loose outside my shorts, I was horrified to see that the groin area of my shorts was dyed red. Inside, I was covered in blood. Two leeches, dangling from my scrotum, had feasted on the blood supply to my private parts. I could only laugh at the thought of them swinging back and forth as I trod through the jungle, unaware that that they were gorging themselves on the lifeblood of my family jewels. But once they were gone, the blood kept on flowing, like water from a tap. What if I became weak through loss of blood and fainted? Then they would all descend on me and suck every last drop out of me. This was no time to start panicking and I regained my self-composure. I hoped I had plenty of blood left, but what a mess I was in.

Soon after we emerged from the jungle, we found a small restaurant by the roadside as we made our way back to the bunkhouse. We were hungry and went in, dripping with sweat, and mud, and blood, and ordered food and drink. The other diners regarded us with some bemusement/distaste/disgust: choose a word, any one will do. As I supped my cool, fresh orange juice, I heard gasps of horror from the group at the next table. Wide-eyed with amazement, and speechless, their fingers were pointing at my left foot. A big, fat leech was squirming its way out of my sock. I bent down, picked it up, and took it over to let them see it.

Panic! Chairs were pushed aside, and folk fled from me as if I were diseased. I can take a hint. I won't stop where I'm not wanted. I took it to the door and threw it out, then went back to my chair and supped my juice again. The diners returned to their seats too.

I thought I'd better check to see if there were any more, and took off my boot. Two more fatties emerged. I deposited the leeches outside once more, then took my sock off, and another two were still in there, feasting on my ankle. They are so flexible that even when walking they just get squeezed in and out like a soft balloon and get fatter and fatter till they decide to leave. My sock was saturated in blood, but I put it back on to help contain the flow that was turning the floor of the restaurant bright red, and used the serviettes on the table to soak the blood up.

I then checked my right boot. There were two in there as well. Paul had managed to dig a couple out from his footwear. Our herd of leeches started hopping across the restaurant floor towards the other tables, clearing a crowd of diners before them like a tsunami. As we were seated right by the entrance, people were clawing at each other to get out by the back door. No one would come near us. I looked quizzically at Paul. "Do we have a body odour problem?"

I put my boots on again, and our food was delivered. The waitress took the salt from the table and poured some on each of the leeches. They shrivelled up. She brought a brush and swept them out. Peace was restored, but few people would sit anywhere near us after that.

Back at the bunkhouse, I struggled to get the bleeding to stop. After showering, I put on a dressing and taped it all round with surgical tape to make a seal. I lay back on the bed with my leaky legs propped up on my rucksack. Gravity helped reduce the flow, and after some time it dried up. I suffered no ill effects.

The leeches may even have had a positive effect. With all their anticoagulant in my blood I had no fear of developing deep vein thrombosis during the flight back to Kota Kinabalu the following day.

You can always find something positive, if you look at things the right way. I had enjoyed my time on Borneo and a year later I was back, this time to dive one of the world's most renowned dive locations.

Chapter 21

SIPADAN

The aircraft soared into the clear, morning sky above Kota Kinabalu. I looked out of the window and there, soaring high above the jungle-clad surrounding hills, was the towering bulk of Mount Kinabalu. I gazed in wonder. Did I really climb to the top of that, clambering up those steep, slab-sided flanks in total darkness, with only a small head-torch and a rope to aid me? Then I was focused only on the few feet ahead or above me as I climbed, gasping for air, unable to see anything of the mountain in the darkness. When you are on a mountain, even in daylight, you rarely get an overall impression of the scale of the thing. Now, I could see this majestic mountain from sea level to summit, all 13,435 feet (4095 metres) of dense green lower slopes, and the sun-scorched, bare rock of its peaks. Its enormity impressed me. Seeing a mountain from the air is a great way to gauge the scale of it, and I felt a glow of satisfaction that I had been able to climb it.

My destination was Pulau Sipadan, a small offshore island described by Jacques Cousteau as *'one of nature's finest works of art.'* I landed at Tawau in the northeastern corner of this huge island. A minibus took me to Semporna, and a fast boat to Borneo Divers' Mabul Resort, where I would be staying.

Mabul Beach

No one is allowed to stay on Sipadan, a tiny island perched on top of a pinnacle of rock that rises from the ocean floor. Its walls are festooned with corals, sponges, anemones, and an impressive variety of marine creatures make their home there. The drop-off is remarkable. Swim out from the beach about ten metres, and you find yourself over a sub-sea cliff that drops almost sheer to the ocean floor 600 metres (1,966 feet) below. You allow yourself to drop down to around 30 metres depth (about 100 feet), and gaze in wonder at the strange creatures living in this submarine tower block. This is high density population, every hole a residence of fish, shrimps, lobster, octopus, resting sharks sleeping after a night's hunting, or sleeping turtles, exhausted after laying several dozen eggs in a hole dug in the sand on the shore.

The number of turtles was astonishing. At first the camera was clicking away, but after seeing dozens of them, you scarcely give them a glance. White-tip reef sharks were abundant, with a few grey reef sharks cruising in the deep water. At one site, aptly named Barracuda Point, the barracuda, sleek and fast for effective hunting and with a vicious set of teeth, schooled in their hundreds above us. Like a cloud passing overhead, they blotted out the light.

The drop off was a favourite place for seeing a huge school of jacks, big-eyed trevally. They swirled around like the cloud that forms in a tornado, with a clear hole in the centre where the diver can enter and hover within this mass of fish circling around him, packed together, going nowhere. From underneath this tower of fish, it is like looking up a chimney to the light far above. They go round in circles all day long, but at night they split up to hunt and become sleek, fast, killers.

I'd had an unfortunate experience with the agency that booked the diving for me. They had promised me six days at Mabul resort, but it could only accommodate me for two nights. I had to spend two nights at two other resorts nearby, but still had to go back for my food and diving with Borneo Divers. The agency had known of this since I booked over two months before, but had fixed this hotch-potch arrangement and did not tell me until two days prior to my arrival.

I was not happy: blazin' mad would be more a accurate description. The resort staff were faultless and expressed their regret that my stay had been spoiled by this inconvenience. When I left I was astonished at their farewell. The boys came out from the dive centre, and the girls from the restaurant. Some who were on the late shift even gave up their free time to come to say goodbye. The manager and reception staff came and shook my hand, and even the managing director's wife came out specially to see me off.

They all asked me to come back, and I did, with Mr-Ray-from-the-USA, Ray Casavant, a gentleman (well, that is perhaps an overstatement!) of similar vintage to myself, whom I had met in the Philippines on the Tubbataha reef live-aboard.

Our first few minutes underwater were enough to justify its claim to be among the top dive spots in the world. We found ourselves among the dense, swirling school of thousands of big-eyed trevally, attracting the photographers and videographers among us. But that was upstaged by another of Sipadan's star turns. Behind the swirling mass, our guide Maadil, pointed over to the reef. Hovering above it was the biggest school of bumphead parrotfish I have ever seen, dozens of them, milling around over the coral. These Frankensteins of the sea, with their distorted bumped foreheads, have the most impressive front teeth. Chisel-like, they are ideal for crunching the hard coral which is their diet. Like so many inhabitants of Sipadan's walls and reefs, the bumpheads tolerate the presence of the diving paparazzi with their clicking cameras.

Bumphead Parrotfish

For those who get a buzz of excitement from seeing sharks, white tip reef sharks and grey reef sharks abound, with the odd hammerhead wandering around too. Usually resting after a night's hunting, they are not aggressive. Timid is a more apt description of most sharks.

After the first morning's dive, we emerged, glistening wet in the morning sun. The surface of the sea was like silk. To my right, the colour was a pale turquoise, where the sunlight was reflected back from the sandy bottom of a shallow bay; to my left it was a deep azure, where the reef edge dropped in that dramatic, sheer wall to the floor of the Celebes Sea.

"How was that, John?" called out Maadil, our dive guide. I spat the regulator out of my mouth.

"Great," I called back.

Ray had more to say. He always does, and waxed eloquently about its wondrous charms. Mind you, he waxes eloquently about everything. He only stops talking when he is underwater, or asleep, and even then not always.

"Now I know what the world was like before mankind started to destroy what nature had created. It was like being in an underwater Garden of Eden."

That is the kind of effect Sipadan can have on people. An Italian I met on my previous visit, remarked in awed tones, "When you see Sipadan, your life changes."

We also explored the waters around Mabul, and Kapalai, a reef and sand bank with a resort built on stilts. It has a number of artificial reefs made from sunken bamboo frames, scrap iron, and old tyres that attract fish, providing shelter from predators. Motionless and well camouflaged on the bottom, lay several large crocodile fish. Members of the sea scorpion family, the long crocodile-like snout gives them their name. Their eyes are fascinating, with what appears to be lace-curtain eyelids. I imagine that is for camouflage, making them less detectable. They are an irresistible attraction for close-up photography.

Crocodile fish

Another star turn was a giant moray eel, holed up in a pile of scrap metal and old tyres. It had its mouth open, while a small cleaner shrimp was busy cleaning the eel's teeth. This is a good example of a symbiotic relationship; the eel gets its dental care, and the shrimp feeds on the scraps of fish it picks from the teeth. What the northern shores of these small islands lack in colourful corals, they make up for in interesting subjects for the photographer.

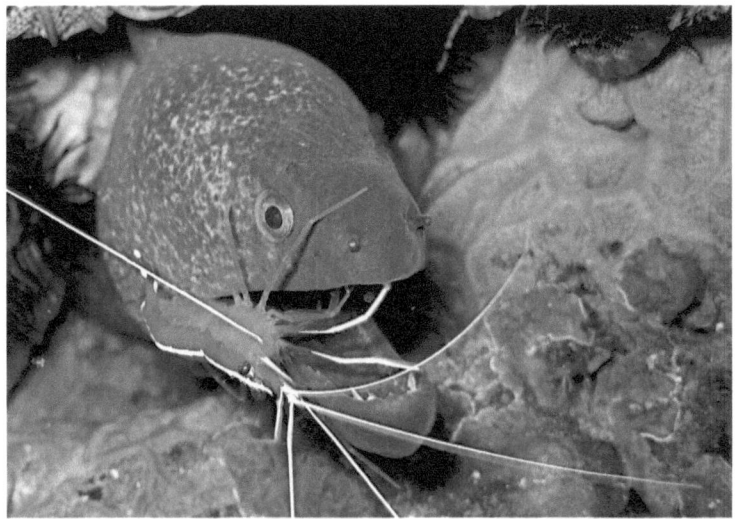

Cleaner Shrimp

Adjacent to our resort on Mabul, were two fishing villages. Water is still pumped out of the ground by hand, and in such a low island it is pretty brackish. A generator supplies electricity, but only at night. The houses are as simple as it is possible to be: a single room perched on stilts, the air circulating underneath keeping them cool. Furniture is non-existent. The people sit on the floor; they sleep on the floor; they eat on the floor. Family planning is an alien concept. Hordes of children play on what passes for streets; no more than narrow gaps between the houses on the sandy beach. These are some of the sea gypsy tribes of South East Asia. While the men travel to fish, the women and children stay put, living out their simple lives on the shore.

Ray and I provided some entertainment as the Odd Couple, two old farts who argued and insulted each other. The resort organised a barbecue and party on the beach, with a few silly games thrown in for fun, one of which was musical chairs. Ray and I were the last two competitors. Dive buddies we may be, but when it came to winning a game of musical chairs there was no love lost, no quarter given, no gentlemanly give and take. This was war: a savage battle for possession of the last chair. My technique was to use a seductive Polynesian dance style around the chairs with knees bent and hips swaying – imagine me in a grass skirt, with half coconut shells covering the boobs. It mesmerised the opposition, and had the added advantage that it kept my backside closer to the chair, so when the music stopped I had less distance to travel.

Sea Gypsy house

Ray's approach was brute force and ignorance. He lacks subtlety. He had already broken the legs of one chair in competition with a large Chinese guy, the two of them rolling about on the grass still clutching the chair to their backsides.

In the final, when my cheeks hit that chair first, (though he disputes that, of course) Ray's ice hockey style barging managed to force one cheek of mine off by virtue of his weight advantage. The man has no finesse, only brute force, but I clung on with the other cheek, my right leg providing a strut that buttressed my claim. Bum to bum, we fought it out, two pensioners fighting like tigers, in a territorial struggle for one chair – and the audience loved it. The management realised that the only way to restore peace was by awarding us each a prize.

An American lady afterwards told me, "I loved your dance style, John. It was very entertaining. But I have never seen two grown men getting so competitive over a chair!"

"Grown men?" Ray exploded. "We haven't grown up yet! We're still kids."

The flight from Tawau back to Kota Kinabalu started well enough with pleasant sunny skies all the way across Borneo. As we approached KK, one side offered a view of Mount Kinabalu, but on the other side the sky was a wall of ominous, dark cloud, illuminated by flashes of lightning. And underneath that was Kota Kinabalu, where we had to connect with our flight to Manila.

The plane veered away from the thunderstorm and flew out over the sea. The intercom crackled: "This is the captain speaking. I am sorry to report that, due to bad weather over Kota Kinabalu, no planes are being allowed to land or take off. We are being diverted to Brunei until the thunderstorm over Kota Kinabalu passes on, but we will get you back as soon as we can."

"As soon as we can…." My heart sank. That vagueness was not encouraging. We arrived back from Brunei as our flight for Manila was taxi-ing out to the runway. Budget airlines don't wait around for latecomers, so we had to buy tickets for the next flight to Manila the following afternoon. That's the travelling life for you.

Travelling with Ray is fun (in a masochistic sort of way!). He expressed a fascination in everything he saw with a wide-eyed look of curiosity, but he is a compulsive talker and I often implored him, with my usual rustic charm, "Ray! Shut up!" I actually miss him – but not a lot! – and our arguments provided plenty of laughs for the others with whom we mingled. However, he is a less sophisticated traveller and I had to teach him a few tricks when flying with budget airlines.

Number one is to travel light. Why do Americans carry so much baggage? I had my dive kit as check-in baggage, but all the rest of my personal stuff for six months travelling fits into my carry-on bag, with room to spare. Ray was abroad for only a month, and appeared with a convoy of bags on wheels, plus a carry-on backpack that was almost twice the permitted carry-on weight. This led to some interesting or, more accurately, confusing discussions at check-in desks about excess baggage costs. No two airlines, or airports, seem to apply the same rules, and Ray had a permanent look of bewilderment. But that is normal for him.

Budget airlines don't board flights according to seat number. It's a free-for-all, unless you have paid extra to select a seat. This is inconvenient if you are near the end of the queue. Many people carry more cabin baggage than they should, and you may find you can't get space in an overhead locker for your hand luggage near your seat. I like to keep my laptop close at hand. However, Air Asia announced priority boarding for adults with young children and the *elderly and infirm*. Ray is proud of his youthful good looks and excellent physique, which make him look twenty years younger than he is – *his* words, not mine – so I had to demand a significant change of image when we found ourselves at the end of a long queue at the departure gate.

I hissed at him: "Ray, do exactly as I tell you. For once, act your age. Droop your head, let your shoulders sag, shuffle your feet and *limp*, like this, and don't say a word!" And I did a good demonstration of the elderly and infirm who would get priority boarding as I shuffled, limping and dragging my left foot across the floor behind me, clutching at his arm for support, and gasping my way to the front of the queue.

Approaching the girl at the gate, I said in a tremulous voice, "Elderly and infirm?" Without hesitation, she waved us through with another elderly, stooping, drooping, and shuffling couple who clutched each other for support. As we walked across the apron to the aircraft, I stepped out briskly and said, "See, that's all it takes."

Ray exploded, "Well, I've seen it all now! You talk about me?" He was spluttering for words. "You are the biggest bullshit merchant ever. You hirpled up to that gate like you would never even make it to the aircraft, and look at you now, stepping out like a teenager. What are all those people in the queue gonna be thinking now?"

"Who cares? We're first on the plane."

He shook his head and chuckled, "Well, this trip has been an education for me." And when we entered the aircraft cabin, who did we find smiling a warm welcome, but the same charming flight attendant who'd served us on our outward flight to Borneo. Air Asia have the most attractive female flight attendants. It is worth taking a flight just to get a look at them.

Ray beamed at her. "How nice to see you again! You know, I called the chief executive of Air Asia and insisted that I wanted *you* on our return flight to take care of us once again."

Bullshit merchant!

"Well, thank you, sir. I look forward to being of service to you again," she said, and nurtured his unbridled lust with a dazzling smile and a fetching giggle.

He held every inch of his sixty-eight year-old youthful physique erect as he strode up the aisle behind me, smirking and mimicking her voice: "I look forward to being of service to you once again, sir. D'ya hear that? Yes please, Ma'am! Elderly and infirm? Huh."

As usual, he managed to get the last word.

And the first.

And most of the words in between!

Chapter 22

SPEAKING PIDGIN

Ba-boooom... booom... boom... ba-boom... It went on for several seconds. It couldn't be the rumble of an approaching thunderstorm. Not on a cloudless, sunny day. Not when your ears are 30 metres below the surface of the sea. It couldn't have been dynamite fishing. That would have been one big bang. Yet it continued to rumble in waves, like a giant beast expressing its anger that divers should invade its territory deep in the Solomon Islands.

It seemed to be coming from behind me. I turned to satisfy my curiosity, hovering in a vertical position, full frontal towards the direction of the sound. A shock wave hit me, accompanied by another deep rumbling explosion. It felt as though a large hand, the size of a dinner plate, had thumped me on the chest. My body reeled from the blow. My ears felt the pressure wave. Something big was happening out there in the blue void. We carried on diving, and the rumbling subsided.

Back aboard the dive boat, Bilikiki, all was explained. It was a large undersea volcano erupting. Its cone was just below the surface of the ocean, 60 miles to the west of our position. It was my first encounter with the effects of an underwater eruption. I admit that, after feeling the shock wave and listening to the undersea explosions,

I was quite happy to be 60 miles away. We were told it throws up huge plumes of water, like a geyser, but 60 miles distant on a hazy day there was no chance of seeing that.

MV Bilikiki

Most of the population of the Solomon Islands are Melanesian, with the characteristic dark skin and fuzzy hair. I was surprised to see a significant proportion of the population with fair hair, not what you would expect of such dark-skinned people, but it is natural, the result of a certain gene. A few thousand Polynesians, that race of great ocean navigators who inhabit so many of the other South Pacific Islands, settled on six of the Solomon Islands, adding an additional strand to the gene pool. On anchoring close to a village, we were greeted by a flotilla of dugout canoes, paddled out from the shore by women and children, curious to see us and sell us some local produce. Rafts of canoes tied up alongside Bilikiki and kept the ship supplied with fresh fruit and vegetables.

On a cultural visit to one village, the local men performed some warrior dances for us. We were advised to dress conservatively, as an ostentatious display of bare skin was likely to offend. That was a wee bit ironic, for we were then entertained by some warriors clad only in the briefest of loincloths who offered more than a glimpse of bare-assed cheek as they pranced around covered in war-paint, knocking axes aggressively against their shields.

Unusual to see fair hair & dark skin

In contrast to the almost naked men, the ladies danced demurely, wearing ankle-length dresses, a style of dress imposed by European missionaries of the 19th and early 20th century. Bare breasts were banned. They claimed it was sinful to expose the female body, and insisted on this incongruous fashion, a style more suitable for a cold European climate than the steamy humidity of the Solomons.

In a land of headhunters where cannibalism was practised until the late 1800s, Christianity and the British influence in establishing laws, medical care, and education have had some benign effects. Religion has a significant influence in the villages. Every morning and evening, the villagers assemble in the meeting-house under the leadership of the chief for prayers. Housing was simple, constructed from bamboo and woven dried leaves.

The most thrilling dive was in a narrow channel with a fierce current running, so powerful that it whipped off my mask as I rolled off the boat and entered the water. I managed to catch it before it was whisked away into the gloom, dived for the bottom where I hooked on, and managed to get the mask back on my face and cleared of water. I drifted along on the current until I met up with the rest of the group, clinging to the reef by the side of the deep channel. These were conditions that attract manta rays. For an hour, we watched nine large mantas perform an aquatic ballet, as they fed on the plankton brought to their cavernous mouths by the current.

An abundance of relics of the Second World War lie around the Solomons, on land and on the seabed. The Japanese built an airfield on Guadalcanal, from which they could harass the sea routes between Australia and the USA, but left it poorly defended and were taken by surprise when the US Marines made an amphibious assault and captured the airfield after only a couple of days. The Japanese counter-attacked in a land, air, and seaborne campaign, each side suffering heavy losses in ships, aircraft and men.

World War II crashed aeroplane engine

The sea between Guadalcanal and Savo, where the US Navy suffered its worst combat defeat in the Pacific, is now littered with the wrecks of US, Japanese, Australian, and New Zealand ships and planes, and is now called Ironbottom Sound. That defeat forced the US Navy to withdraw support for the marines ashore on Guadalcanal for a time. Despite this setback, the marines overcame odds of three to one to maintain control of the airfield, their only lifeline. The

Japanese lost 33,000 men, the Americans 7,000 in six months of intense fighting, until the Japanese withdrew.

Abandoned tanks, guns, vehicles, and parts of aircraft can be encountered almost anywhere, and the shoreline is littered with the rusting hulls of ships, bombed or torpedoed, and run ashore to try to salvage whatever could be saved of their cargoes. The American War Memorial is an informative testimony to the young men who gave their lives in the struggle, but the Japanese Memorial is vandalised with graffiti. It is used as a drinking den by young people, with broken beer bottles littering the area.

Most divers who come here fly in, embark on Bilikiki to dive, and fly out again on the day they disembark. Few stay around to have a look at the place. I came eight days early to have a taste of Solomon Islands life with the irrepressible Mr-Ray-From-The-USA Casavant. We had laughs chatting with the waitresses and housekeeping staff, practising the language, and entertaining them with our heated arguments. Few tourists spent time talking to them, they told us, so the word spread that if you want a laugh, go and talk to "the boys in triple 1" (our hotel room, 111). It became a daily routine for the housemaids to sit in our room for ten minutes or so, chatting with us and having a laugh, before cleaning the room and making the beds.

Each night at dinner, we were entertained to some music by Robert, a gifted guitarist. He invited me to accompany him with my hand-crafted wooden spoons. The effect was interesting. A group of noisy Australians at the bar stopped talking, bottles of beer suspended halfway to their lips, mouths open in anticipation. Out came the chef and the kitchen staff, in came the security guards and the receptionist from the front desk to listen. When we finished playing, I was called up to the bar to show the Australians the kind of instrument I was playing.

"Where can I buy one of these?" asked one of the Aussies.

"As far as I know, there is only one man in the world who makes these," I said.

"How do I get in touch with him?"

"You are talking to him right now." I showed him two spare sets I was carrying with me. Both were sold there and then, and that paid my hotel bill for the week. I wished I'd had time to make more before I left home.

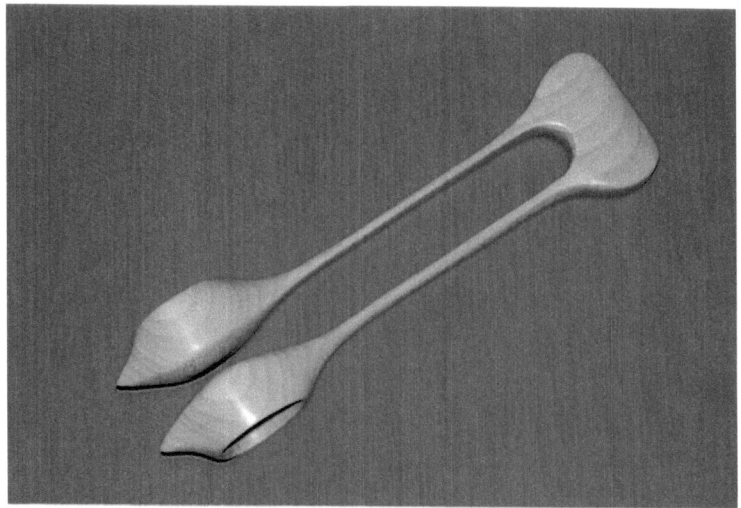

Hand-made spoons for percussion

Over 900 different languages are used in the Solomon Islands, each with little in common with the others. Few people can speak any of these other than their own. This created problems for government, education, trade, and commerce. There are only two approved official languages, English and Pidgin, a peculiar phonetic lingua franca devised by traders in the 1800s to facilitate their dealings with Pacific islanders. It is used, with regional variations, not only in the Solomon Islands, but also in Papua New Guinea, Vanuatu, and Hawaii. A universal language seemed the best way forward, and this peculiar version of English found acceptance. It is a delight to learn and is very descriptive.

"I am very pleased to meet you" in Pidgin is: Mi hapi tumas fo mitim yu. Now listen to the sound of that, and the meaning becomes clear. Mi hapi tumas = me happy too much, meaning, I am very pleased; fo mitim yu = for meeting you. Makes sense doesn't it?

Tanggio tumas = Thank you too much = Thank you very much.

Wat nau nem blong yu? = Literally, what now name belong you? = What is your name?

Nem blong mi, John = My name is John.

Lukim yu behine = See you later. Literally, looking you behind. (If something comes behind it will be *later* than what comes first). Get it?

Or in Pidgin, Yu savvy? = You know? or Do you understand?

I loved talking this language. Even more so when the waitresses in the hotel were delighted that I should want to learn more, and greeted me each morning at breakfast with a big smile and said, "Naes fo lukim yu, John" (nice for looking you, John = nice to see you, John) and gave me a lingering hug. And they were queuing up to do it too!

To which I replied, "Tanggio tumas. Mi hapi tumas fo lukim yu." (Thank you very much. I am very pleased to see you). Well, who wouldn't be with a welcome like that each morning? Yes, mi hapi tumas!

However, dis fella sitim hea ritim tumas, so nomoa. Mi go baeleg. Lukim yu behine!

Yu savvy?

This fellow is sitting here writing too much, so no more. I am going for a walk. See you later. You understand?

Chapter 23

EARTHQUAKES GALORE

The volcanic landscape of New Britain was revealed as my flight emerged from the clouds above Kimbe Bay, my destination. The wide bay, once the caldera of an ancient volcano now filled by the sea, is sprinkled with reefs presenting a kaleidoscope of colours to brighten the dark blue of the ocean. The plane swung out over the sea on its final approach, offering an alluring glimpse of what was in store for me.

Well, some of what was in store for me.

The earth moved at 3 a.m. The bed was bouncing, but it wasn't caused by a night of passion. It was an earthquake. There is much to be said for simple methods of construction where earthquakes are common. My bungalow was constructed of bamboo and thatch. Easy and quick to build, their capability to flex helps them survive when concrete houses crack and fall. Even if the roof fell in on me, I didn't think it would do too much damage. It was only thatch tied to bamboo purlins. Reluctant to get up at that hour, I lay in bed and shook until the quake subsided. After a few more tremors lasting only a few seconds, all became quiet again.

In the eight days I stayed on New Britain, we had six earthquakes, all between 4.8 and 5.8 on the Richter scale. No serious structural damage was caused, but they managed to put the phones out of order for three days, and the internet was down. Some happened while I was diving, but the effect in the sea was insignificant, just a low rumble.

You get used to the earth shuddering as you walk along, leaves shaking on trees, buildings swaying. The locals didn't bother. Why should I? When they occurred at night, I lay in bed, listening to the bottles and cans in the fridge dancing with each other until it passed. It is part of daily life, and I was soon asleep again.

New Britain lies to the north of Papua and is part of the state of Papua New Guinea. Located on an active geological fault line, earthquakes and volcanic eruptions are common. The island is a series of volcanic peaks, many of which are dormant, but in 1994, an eruption destroyed Rabaul, the provincial capital. Propelled thousands of metres into the air, a rain of ash caused 80% of the buildings in Rabaul to collapse under its weight. But the people are persistent. Despite several trashings in the 20th century, they continue to rebuild Rabaul.

At Kimbe Bay, we had a volcano almost in our backyard. From time to time it threw up plumes of smoke and hydrogen sulphide gas which, being denser than air, rolled down the mountainside when the wind was from the south and engulfed us in the awful stench of rotten eggs. This evil smelling, toxic gas, could be smelt three miles out at sea. However, most of the time the wind was from the north, blowing the smell away from us.

The diving was very good, with a wide variety of subjects for photography, notably my first shot of a Hippocampus denise, a species of pygmy seahorse. Living on fan corals, these tiny animals, blending so well with the colour and texture of the coral strands, are very difficult to find. It takes a guide with a keen eye and good knowledge of his environment to find them.

The boat trips to the numerous reefs also offered opportunities to watch whales and dolphins. To allow us to view the dolphins underwater, the boat crew slung booms over the side, aft of the bow, with heavy cargo netting attached. Wearing mask and snorkel, we jumped over the side and attached ourselves to the netting with hands and feet.

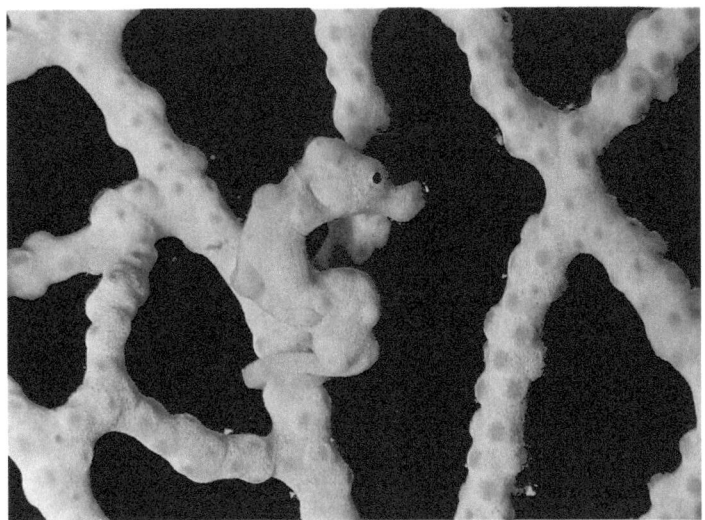

Pygmy seahorse: Hippocampus denise

Travelling at a modest 5 knots to keep the dolphins interested in playing in our bow pressure wave, you need to lock your feet into the net. It was almost impossible to hang on using arms only. I managed to hang on with two feet and one hand, the other hand operating my small camera underwater to get some pictures of the dolphins jostling for position in the bow wave. Those with large cameras found it impossible.

Dolphins playing in the bow wave

The sounds of the jungle at night are fascinating. Walking to and from the main building for dinner each evening, the ever-present chatter of thousands of insects in the trees calling to one another with that peculiar castanet sound as they rattle parts of their body together, calling for a mate, was at times deafening. Large frogs were everywhere, dark silent blobs jumping out of my way on the path that wound through the trees. My hair and face were covered in the silky filaments of spiders' webs by the time I had walked the 200 metres to the restaurant.

At the end of my visit, a minibus took me back to the airfield. Built by the Japanese during World War II, it had not been modernised since then. The runway had no lighting, which is awkward if the afternoon flight from Port Moresby, the capital of Papua New Guinea, has been delayed and arrives over the airfield towards dusk on a cloudy evening. If the pilot reckons it will be too dark to give him a clear view of the runway by the time he offloads his passengers and picks up those waiting below, he won't land and turns back to Port Moresby. That gives the inbound passengers a 3-hour round trip from Port Moresby and back, and the outward bound passengers have to seek lodgings in New Britain for another night. It is advisable to build in some latitude when booking connecting flights to allow for delays and last-minute cancellations.

The skies were clear for me, the flight was on time, and I managed to get back to Port Moresby with plenty of time for my connection to Brisbane.

Chapter 24

THAILAND

Thailand, land of smiles, sounds, and smells unlike anything I had ever experienced, is a charming country. For my first visit, I had booked adventure travel tours to both north and south Thailand. Having a guide for a first visit to a country with an unfamiliar language is a good idea. After that, I was able to return and travel independently with ease. Its bustling, modern cities have streets thronged with people and market traders who sell cooked food, meat, fish, vegetables, spices, clothes, sculptures, paintings, trinkets, indeed just about anything that can be sold. In some places, the bicycle powered rickshaw still competes for passengers with the motor taxi and the ubiquitous tuk-tuk, a tiny bus. Modernity and tradition sit cheek-by-jowl in most places.

The smells are distinctive, not only the spices and delicious food, but also the drains. Eating food outside is a delight in the evening, but not if you are downwind of an evil-smelling drain. Have a sniff around first to check that no offensive effluvium is likely to drift your way.

Fantastic, incredible, beautiful, are only some of the words to describe the Thai Buddhist temples with the golds, whites, reds, blues, and greens of the detailed decoration of their bizarre architecture glinting in the sunlight. Around them, shaven-headed Buddhist monks wearing saffron robes add another distinctive dash of colour.

Thai Temple

After a day's sightseeing in Bangkok, we headed north for two weeks to trek, stay in primitive villages with hill tribes, and explore rivers by kayak and barge. First stop was Kanchenaburi on the River Kwai, where the famous Bridge Over The River Kwai was built during World War II. The bridge carried the so-called death railway to aid the Japanese expansion westwards through Thailand and Burma towards India. Built not only by allied prisoners of war, but also by tens of thousands of Thai and Burmese civilians, the dreadful conditions, malnutrition, and cruelty of the regime under which they worked, resulted in the deaths of over 300,000 people. The famous bridge, immortalised in literature and film, is now a magnet for tourists, a monument to those who died there. The bridge was never destroyed, as depicted in the film of the same name. Hollywood likes to make its own versions of history.

A two-day river trip, on a former rice barge converted to carry passengers, offered glimpses of life on the river. Along its banks, people live and work, fish and play, do their laundry and bathe themselves in it, while the river traffic, enormous barges towed by small tugs, ploughs past. The barge people live a nomadic life, living on their barges, going wherever cargo is to be taken. I loved the bustle and variety and colour of it. And on land we explored villages by bicycle and gained glimpses of rural life.

Bridge Over River Kwai

A visit to Ayutthaya, once the ancient capital of Siam, was followed by a trip north to Chang Mai and Chang Rai. While waiting for the northbound train, I wandered along the station platform, wearing my kilt. Passing two Japanese girls, seated on their rucksacks, one of them looked up at me. Her eyes seemed to carry a message which I interpreted as, 'I'd like you to talk to me,' and her eyes lit up with a wee smile. I smiled aback and said "Hello." She responded, and we engaged in conversation. Both architecture students, they hoped to come to Europe to study architecture, and after I let them see some pictures I had on my laptop, they decided a visit to Scotland had to be included. The young men in our group watched this for a few minutes, then came over and asked to be introduced. One of the boys muttered in my ear, "John, how the hell do you do it? You're only here two minutes and you're already chatting up two beautiful girls."

After dining had ended on the overnight train to Chiang Mai, the dining car became the 'party car' for backpackers. It served drinks, with background music. When Sam, our Thai guide, insisted I play the spoons, the party really took off. Brits were dancing with French, Austrians with Italians, and the Thai waitresses were dancing with everyone as they served the drinks.

Rice barges

That night, my beloved wooden spoons became a casualty. I am always happy to let people try them, but one of our group became a bit wild, struck them the wrong way, and broke them. My heart sank. These spoons had been round the world five times with me. It was touching to see the looks on everyone else's face. They scowled at the lad who had broken them, and came over to console me as though a death had occurred. The lad who'd broken them felt terrible and apologised. However, that forced me to try to make a set when I returned home, and I have been making and selling them ever since.

Two days later in Chiang Mai, while walking to an open-air restaurant wearing my kilt, I heard a cry, "John!" It was the two Japanese girls again, and they joined me for dinner. At the next table were four Vietnamese people who had been attending an educational conference. Soon they too were deep in conversation with us and asked if they could take photographs. As I stood in the middle of the group for a photo, I heard a voice from a table behind me: "Look at him!" The rest of our travel group had arrived. "You've done it again, John. Wherever you go you seem to make friends so easily. How do you do it?"

I don't know, but who cares? It's one of the pleasures of travel. But wearing a kilt does help!

A trek through jungle, up and over mountains, took us to the hill tribe people of the Akha and Lisu tribes who live in traditional huts made of bamboo and thatch. The huts have neither windows nor a chimney to let the smoke from the cooking fires escape. It drifts out through the door, or any other space it can find, as the structures are only loosely put together. Their fields, won from the forest, grow vegetables, coffee, and fruit.

Having migrated from Tibet and China to Myanmar, these tribes moved into Thailand about a hundred years ago. They wear distinctive clothing, of a style more appropriate to the climate of Tibet than the tropics, but it is cooler high up in the mountains. In the evenings, children performed traditional songs and dances around a campfire. At the village school, we were invited to teach them English, and play games with them outside.

Akha Tribe woman

Traditional Akha dance

Following our return to Bangkok we headed south to experience what southern Thailand had to offer: beautiful beaches, spectacular islands, great food, warm sea, superb diving. The night train from Bangkok to southern Thailand proved to be just as entertaining as the train north had been. Wan, the charming Thai girl who was our tour leader for this southern part of the trip, asked in her delightful accent, "John, you want to go to Pahtee Cah?" Having been briefed by our previous guide, she knew what to expect and we had another lively evening in the party car. This time, I borrowed a couple of soup spoons from the train's kitchen.

From Surat Thani we moved on by road to the Khao Sok National Park to stay in bamboo raft houses for a couple of days. These were constructed on floating rafts on a huge lake amidst stunning scenery. The landscape is predominantly limestone, with precipitous cliffs soaring out of the lake and jungle. Limestone caves abound and we explored underground, as well as on the lake, and in the jungle.

Our local jungle guide demonstrated how to swing on a vine, Tarzan style, and then challenged anyone to try it. I was first to volunteer, but he said, "No, John. You too old. Need to be stlong to do this. Too dangelous fo' you." Thais have difficulty pronouncing the letter R. It comes out as L. I gave him a withering look and grabbed the vine.

Khao Sok Lake

"Havers," I retorted, and before he could drag it back from me I was off, swinging out over the gully below, like Tarzan. It was a long vine, giving me a leisurely glide over the gully and back again to cheers from the rest of the group.

That changed the guide's tune. "Oh John, you vely stlong man," he gushed, feeling my biceps.

"Aye, and don't you forget it!" I growled back at him, with a grin.

On an evening boat trip on the lake, high up on a cliff about 300 feet high, a black cloud emerged, but it was not smoke – it was bats. Thousands of big fruit bats, about the size of a chicken, poured out of the cave for their nocturnal feed. It was an amazing sight as they headed east in a column about thirty bats wide.

Also on the lake was a floating bar. It was accessed by a raft, connecting shore and bar by a rope, which you pulled to take yourself across. The barmaid was a beautiful girl from Croatia who had fallen in love with one of the Thai lads who worked there. She was an asset to the bar, and our young lads were happy to spend all day there feasting their eyes on her, supping cold beer to cool their ardour. At night, lying on our backs on the raft, we gazed at the myriad of stars in a sky unpolluted by artificial light, and talked about philosophy, the nature of the universe, and all the things that star-gazing and a few Singa beers bring to mind.

The next location was some jungle huts in an area where tigers and elephants still roam wild, where poisonous snakes, notably the King Cobra, slither among the trees, and where monkeys chatter among the tree tops and come down to the river to drink in the evenings. All that added a touch of excitement when walking to the toilet block in the middle of the night, especially when you find a lizard the size of a small crocodile occupying the toilet. That helped to clear a few bowels. A lot of people would not go to the toilet alone at night.

On our last morning there, Wan, our leader, came down the steps from her hut – they are all on stilts – reached out to grasp the handrail and squealed when she almost placed it on top of a two-metre long green snake which was slithering up the rail. I grabbed my camera and rushed up to photograph it. It had no malicious intent, but it was venomous and was making its way to the roof for a bit of sunbathing. One of the local boys dislodged it with a bamboo pole and it meandered off into the bush. Things like that do make you think about going to the toilet block in darkness.

The south of Thailand has a significant Moslem population, and a homestay with a Thai family near Krabi demanded observance of protocols; long trousers only, no bare shoulders, shoes off before entering the house, no alcohol. The owner took us to demonstrate tapping for rubber in his plantation. He then picked some fresh pineapples for us, and we all sat on the floor to eat a huge dinner his wife and daughters had prepared for us.

The food was excellent, but in one dish of mixed vegetables I swallowed a red-hot chilli which scorched its way down my throat. My stomach felt like a hot coal had entered it, and it burned long into the night. It was about 3 a.m. before the fire within me had subsided to a glow and I could get to sleep. Since then I have been ultra cautious about what I eat, inspecting every morsel for these demonic Thai chillies. We spent a couple of days there, but while the others went shopping, I went diving for the first time in Thai waters. That was enough to convince me I must return.

A couple of hours drive and a short voyage by long-tailed boat took us to Koh Rok, a small island off the west coast where we were to camp for a few days. The so-called long-tailed boats use a conventional diesel engine, but adapted to be more like an outboard engine. Balanced neatly on a cradle near the stern of the boat, it has a long propeller shaft trailing astern, hence the name, long-tailed boat. The boatman can raise or lower the prop out of the water, so finely balanced is the engine, and can swivel it round too. They are handy in shallow waters where they can beach the boat to let people off, raising the propeller out of the water to avoid damage.

Long-tailed boat

On the way out, we stopped below the 300-foot cliffs of Koh Muk, and jumped into the sea. Ahead of us lay the entrance to a cave about eighty metres long. We swam in, following our leader who had a waterproof torch. Deep inside, the cave was in total darkness as it snaked one way, then the other, blanking out any light from the entrance. Rounding another bend, we were confronted by an emerald glow from the water, and a beautiful white beach ahead. Stepping out into the sunshine, we found ourselves on the floor of a huge hole in the limestone, about 100 metres across and 100 metres (300 feet) deep, with vertical sides. The island was shaped like a doughnut. The only access to the beach was by swimming through the tunnel.

Back aboard the boat, a two hour voyage took us to Koh Rok, an island with golden beaches, and all the rustlings and mutterings you hear in a jungle at night. I loved it and slept under the stars for three nights, in a hammock slung between two trees, in preference to lying in a tent, which I found too hot, hard, and stuffy. Insect repellent kept the mosquitos at bay, but it did not stop a lizard from sharing the hammock with me. About a foot long, it was sitting on my chest gazing at me when I woke up.

On our return to Koh Muk, I fitted in another couple of dives. At a big rock pinnacle, we entered an underwater cave teeming with fish. The beam of the torch reflected off the sides of the fish with flashes of silver. A shadowy movement of something big, and a shark made its way off into the darkness. I couldn't stop thinking about the earthquake that caused the tsunami in 2004. What would happen if we had another one while in here, deep in the innards of this great lump of rock. Would we be entombed, or crushed to death? The probability was so slight it was not worth bothering about, so why spoil the day. The cave had a U shape, and when we turned towards the exit, hundreds of fish were silhouetted against the glowing light at the cave mouth, a fitting finale to my first visit to South Thailand.

On the night train to Bangkok, the "Pahtee Cah" did not have the friendly atmosphere we had experienced on the way south. Neither the train staff, nor the other travellers, were in party mood, so I went to my bunk to read. An hour later, I heard voices raised in concern about two of our group who had stayed on, but had drunk too much. They were arguing with the restaurant car staff about being charged for beer they claimed they hadn't drunk. Wan had gone to try to calm things down, but they were too drunk to listen to reason, and she came back disgusted. Confrontation is not respectful in Thai culture. This was an unfortunate way to end what had been a very harmonious trip. I got out of my bed and went along. I didn't like what I saw.

The atmosphere had become tense, verging on ugly. Voices were raised. The language was less than genteel. Five armed railway policemen were standing by watching, as two of our boys tried to persuade the drinkers to leave. A glance round the other faces in the car revealed a lot of tension, with a few ready to lay some punches was my reckoning.

It was a time for swift action: a touch of diplomacy, with firmness, tact, and sensitivity. I grabbed the loud-mouthed guy and pinned him against the wall, whispering sweet words in his ear in a rasping low voice that carried all the menace I could muster, and spelled out what was in store for him if he did not listen to what Papa John was telling him, but done in a loving and caring manner. It worked. I shepherded him back to the sleeping car. With him out of the way, the girl who was with him followed quietly, and we got them both to bed. They offered apologies to the group in the morning. The boy also apologised to the restaurant car staff. It was only then he noticed one of the policemen on board wearing a revolver on his belt, and realised the sense in what I had said the night before. He apologised to the policeman too. Most of the problems experienced by tourists in Thailand are fuelled by drink.

That was the last bit of excitement. It had been fun travelling with them for four weeks. We all got on well, and I still hear the voice of my young, drunk friend offering me the ultimate compliment the morning after: "John, I wish you had been my Dad."

Chapter 25
BIRTHDAY MANTAS

While we were kitting up as the dive boat made passage southwards from Phuket, the dive guide asked: "How old are you, John?"

"Sixty-six today,"

"Oh, so what would you like to see on your birthday dives?"

"Och, a couple of manta rays will do fine."

Open-mouthed Manta Ray

Maybe Poseidon, the god of the sea, was listening. For when we did our second dive that day, two beautiful manta rays circled around us; graceful, elegant, magnificent, flapping their wings slowly and gliding around and above us. One parted a dense school of trevally and came straight towards me with its mouth wide open, giving me the opportunity to take a photo looking straight into that huge mouth. Our guide claimed he had fixed it for my birthday.

Among those who offered birthday good wishes was Lina, a charming flight attendant with Singapore Airlines. We had chatted all the way out on the boat from Phuket, and on hearing the news that it was my birthday, she held my hand, looked into my eyes, and sang Happy Birthday to me, then gave me a wee kiss on the cheek. We exchanged email addresses, and I was delighted several years later when she and her husband and two children came to visit me in Scotland. Arriving back in port at dusk, the sky erupted in a riot of colour and noise as a fireworks display started.

"Hey John, they've fixed up quite a show for your birthday," she joked.

Most of the daily dives from Phuket are among small islands around Koh Phi Phi, and one or two spots in between. The wreck of the car ferry, King Cruiser, is a popular site, not far from a pinnacle of rock called Shark Point. Though still largely intact, the vessel is deteriorating, so penetration is limited to those parts which are safe to enter. The current is strong, and you have to haul yourself down a buoy rope attached to the wreck. As you descend, you may encounter groups of divers clinging to the rope on their way up, having their safety stop at five metres. If you let go, you are liable to be swept away, so you clamber over their bodies, always hanging on with at least one hand.

Shark Point is a beautiful dive consisting of three rock pinnacles. Festooned with beautiful corals and anemones and home to thousands of reef fish, every crevice seemed to have a moray eel's head poking out of it. Sharks and stingrays rested on the sandy bottom between the pinnacles; lion fish performed their slow-motion aquatic ballet, gliding like a bunch of feathers between the rocks.

Anemone Reef, another dive site nearby is well-named. A garden of sea anemones, their tentacles swaying in the current, harbour the cute little Clown Anemone Fish, better known throughout the world as Nemo, from the Disney film. They peek out at you, and with a flick of the tail disappear among the tentacles of the anemone, then show their faces again. Cute they may be, but they become aggressive if you get close when they are guarding eggs, or have their babies, and they are prepared to dart at your face and bite if you don't heed their warnings.

Koh Doc Mai is a dramatic island with vertical rock walls and a cave or two to explore. Small bamboo sharks can be found resting on its ledges, and the walls are a riot of colour. Enormous shoals of small fish swarm together for safety in an opaque mass, hovering and swirling like dark clouds along a mountainside.

The drawback when diving from Phuket is that these sites are often overcrowded. Hundreds of divers go out every morning from Chalong pier. The best value is to take a live-aboard boat for a week. They travel to less crowded islands, and it was on one such boat that I celebrated my 69th birthday.

I did five dives that birthday. Manta rays were there to greet me on all four daytime dives, swooping and soaring, close up and personal, as they cruised around the pinnacles of Hin Daeng and Hin Muang, two memorable dive sites in southern Thai waters. They may have been around during the night dive as well, but in darkness I was focusing my torch on the small animals on the reef.

That trip got off to a slow start. Some of the Phuket streets had been closed to traffic as a parade to celebrate the start of the high season was due at 5 p.m. The diverted traffic resulted in congestion and chaos, and it took our truck 3 hours to travel only 2 kilometres to the jetty at Patong, where we embarked. We then had to wait till another truck, with tanks of nitrox and petrol for the outboard engine on the dinghy, fought its way through the grid-locked traffic. We were scheduled to leave at 5 p.m., and to make a stop at Racha Yai for a night dive on the way south, at around 8 p.m. We were still sitting immobile in traffic at that time. We also had to wait for one diver's baggage. It had failed to arrive on the same flight as he had, but was due to arrive at the airport at 5 p.m. So we waited. And waited. A driver had been sent to rush it through to us. But his 'rush' took until 9.30 p.m. It was 10 p.m. before we got underway, so that ruled out the night dive. However, five dives were planned for the following day. With only five divers on board, the compressors would be able to cope with re-fills of air to accommodate that programme if we started early.

At 6 a.m, we dropped off the stern of the boat in quick succession to explore Hin Daeng. All that showed above the surface of the sea were four fang-toothed rocks without any navigation warning light on them as they were not in a commercial shipping lane. About 300 metres away was Hin Muang, another pinnacle. It does not even break the surface of the ocean, but lurks just underneath. Our skipper had brought us safely to a mooring buoy close by these menacing rocks in the darkness. Nice work.

Dropping down to around 30 metres, we meandered among the gullies and pinnacles of what is a small mountain range. Scenically attractive, these rocks are teeming with fish. Even without the mantas it would have been a good dive, but the mantas made their appearance and mesmerised us, soaring around the pinnacles in a majestic display of effortless power.

It is an awesome sight to see a monster fish, weighing around 1100 kilos (2500 lbs) with a wing span of around 5 metres and jaws a metre wide, banking in a steep turn and coming straight towards you. At any distance they are impressive and awe-inspiring, but when you get monsters of those dimensions so close that you could touch them, they are overwhelming. They seemed to slow down on the approach to have a good look at us, but when it seemed a collision was inevitable, a flick of the wing tip took them soaring overhead, blanking out the sunlight. These were timeless moments, and it took some discipline to check the gauges to make sure we had enough air to see us back to the surface.

Breakfast on board was dominated by animated conversation after that display. It was matched on the second dive at Hin Muang, and on subsequent dives, as we alternated between the two rocks. Having seen it all before, I wandered off on my own to take photos of other things around the pinnacles.

While having lunch, a call came through on the ship's radio from another boat nearby, telling us that a whale shark was cruising around Hin Muang. Having just finished the second dive it would not be safe to dive again so soon, but we did get masks and snorkels on, and the ship's dinghy took us over and dropped us off. And there was the other giant of the deep, a whale shark, the largest fish in the ocean. They grow up to 12 metres long, and at that size it is difficult to get the whole body into the frame of the camera. Cruising around at some depth below us, it was too far away to get a decent photo.

Olivier. Awe struck

I was thrilled, getting all this on my birthday, but Olivier, a young Frenchman who had only 8 dives behind him at the start of the cruise, was witnessing a fantastic display by mantas and a whale shark, something few people see in a lifetime, and all before he had even completed 10 dives. Spoiled brat!

After another morning dive there, with mantas again, the ship was on the move to Koh Haa, a lofty pinnacle of limestone rising sheer from the seabed. As is common with limestone pinnacles, it was honeycombed with inter-connecting chambers and passageways. It would not be difficult to get lost in there, so we had to stick close to the guide.

Making passage back towards Phuket, we dived Koh Bida Nok and Koh Bida Nai, two 'brother' limestone rocks, and Shark Point, after which we returned to Phuket. Hin Daeng and Hin Muang had it all; attractive, colourful, rugged, with as much marine life as you could wish for.

Koh Bida Nok & Koh Bida Nai

Some things you can depend on in Thailand. The food is delicious and inexpensive. You can have a good massage at a low price – and you can depend on having your ego massaged as well!

"You handsome man, velly stlong."

"No, I am an old man now!"

"You no old man! You got powah, good body. You young man."

It is a bit of fun and it makes you feel good. Except that they do it to everyone else, and when you see what some of the others look like, well, it devalues the compliment a bit. But it's worth a tip for the entertainment value.

Chapter 26

LIVING THE DREAM

K oh Bon pinnacle lies 20 metres below sea level, a few hundred metres west of Koh Bon Island, one of the Similan Islands, a string of small rocky islands in the Andaman Sea to the west of Thailand. At 7 a.m. we'd dropped in quick succession off the stern of the dive boat, Jonathan Cruiser, and finned down to avoid being swept past the pinnacle in the strong current.

Sheltering behind the rock to escape the force of the full-moon tide, we watched tunas darting in to feed on the small fry that school there in vast numbers, but it was the mantas that often glide around the peak that were the main attraction. They seemed interested in us as they flew past, swung round, and came back for another look from those strange eyes set far apart on each the side of the wide head.

This is typical of life undersea in the Similan Islands. Each island appears to be a jumble of enormous boulders, rocks piled on top of each other with spaces underneath to swim through. Large, spiny lobsters secrete themselves away in the darker crevices, their presence betrayed by long, white feelers, and in one dark cave no fewer than five white-tipped reef sharks rested in the shade.

Having been on Jonathan Cruiser the year before, I knew what to expect, and coming aboard on the first day I looked into the galley. Mama Lek, our 63 year-old Thai cook, was preparing dinner.

"Hello again, Mama Lek!" I cried.

"Mistah John! You come back!" she squealed with delight. "How are you?"

"Och, I'm fine, but a year older now."

"No! You look same-same last year. You still young man!"

I laughed. "Oh, you are a charmer."

Her eyes narrowed with a mischievous glint. "You still single?"

"Yes, of course."

"OK, I go wit' you." She threw back her head and laughed. I laughed too, but I wonder just how serious she was. She was a marvellous cook. The food was one of the attractions that drew me back four times to this vessel, and each trip offered new experiences.

Jonathan Cruiser could sleep fourteen divers, but on this trip there were only four of us: Mike, Ray, Tony, all from the USA , and me. I had met them on my Tubbataha Reef trip in the Philippines the previous year, and they had asked me to keep in touch. When I mentioned I was heading to the Similan Islands on my next trip, they were all keen to join me. Having the boat to ourselves was great, and it was a joy to dive again with my three experienced buddies. These joint diving trips became annual events, and these three guys have also visited me in Scotland.

Jonathan Cruiser

Mike, Ray, John, Tony

Being eaten alive at the bottom of the sea may not be everyone's idea of fun. No, forget all the baloney about sharks, as portrayed by Hollywood films and storytellers with more imagination than experience. It is the small fish that are hungry for a taste of humans. During an early morning dive, it was a delight to be in clear, warm water, with a temperature of 30 degrees Celsius, taking photos – until I became an item on the menu for some hungry fish. My neck, face, ears, and lips were being being attacked and bitten. Like a scene from a horror movie, a school of remoras, otherwise known as cleaner wrasse, swarmed around my head and attacked me like piranhas. They nibbled away, tearing off dead skin cells from my lips, cheeks, eyebrows, forehead, even scraping out the debris that had gathered in my ears. Cleaning me up, in fact.

I confess hadn't bothered to wash my face before entering the water. It hadn't seemed worth it, for it wasn't long after crawling out of my bunk that I was underwater, so I might as well let the sea do the job for me. And it did, with a vengeance. It wasn't painful, just a series of sharp nips, more amusing than alarming. But before they had all eaten their fill of me, I hit on the idea of turning my camera round, and managed to get a picture of a remora nibbling away at me, proof of my being eaten alive on the seabed. Well, not all of me; only redundant skin cells that would have fallen off anyway for the dust mites to eat. But it was bizarre experience.

Richelieu Rock was one of the places 'discovered' by Jacques Cousteau. Of course, the Thai fishermen already knew it well and took him to it, but they hadn't explored it underwater. He described it as one of the top dive sites in the world. Only visible as a rock above sea level at low tide, this multi-summit pinnacle is a riot of colour. Among its caves and gullies and around its precipitous walls, an amazing diversity of marine life is to be found. You see every colour in the artist's palette. Everything in the ocean seems to gather there, and whale sharks often cruise around it. It is a dive site whose visual impact is such that the camera cannot do it justice.

All sorts of delights lie in wait for you, if you take your time and look carefully, for some do not advertise their presence. Gliding alongside Yay, our dive guide who had signalled to change direction to go with the flow of the current, he grabbed my arm and pulled me towards him. The current was pushing me towards a rock shelf and there, sitting on it, was a large octopus. I was less than an arm's length from experiencing an intimate embrace with it.

It curled its tentacles around it, much as a naked photographic model may do with her legs and arms in order to conceal her private parts. Its skin texture, rough looking to match the texture of the rock, made it almost indistinguishable from its background. Yay had done well to notice it. I raised my camera, and it posed, unconcerned by our close proximity. That is unusual. If you get too near, they begin to flash like a warning light at you, their skin emitting different colours in a threatening display, but this one sat on its perch and modelled for me.

Having completed our last dives at the aptly named Elephant Rock and Boulder City on the way south again, the boat got underway for the overnight journey back to Phuket. As we dined on deck, the ocean was burnished by the light of the setting sun, and later streaked with the silver reflection of the full moon. We could see the approaching mainland before taking to our bunks around midnight. In the early hours of the morning, the engine note changed to a gentle throb as we approached our mooring just off the pier at Chalong, and then fell silent. Another wonderful voyage to the Similan Islands was over.

I love the pattern of life on a live-aboard dive boat: wake up and have a dive before breakfast. Eat breakfast and rest, with another dive before lunch. Eat and rest for an hour or so, followed by an afternoon dive. Enjoy a tasty snack around 4 p.m. A night dive around 7 p.m. is followed by dinner. Relax with a drink, and swap yarns around the table. Sleep. Dive. Eat. Relax in glorious weather, with calm seas and good visibility. Who could ask for more?

I recalled the excellent TV series, *The Undersea World of Jacques Cousteau,* broadcast for several years in the 1960s and 1970s. I watched with envy as Cousteau and his colleagues travelled the world and dived from their converted ex-British minesweeper, Calypso. But at that time I had a wife and two young children to support, a career to manage, a mortgage to pay. I could only dream of such a lifestyle.

It never occurred to me that one day I would explore many of the locations I saw on Cousteau's films. But circumstances change. My sons married. My wife died. I retired. I travelled the world and learned to dive.

I followed my dream.

Chapter 27

IN BED WITH TWO NURSES

You meet interesting characters on live-aboard dive boats. If you are lucky, you may develop a great camaraderie and lasting friendships. But if the dynamics of the group don't work favourably, having to endure the company of people you cannot stand for a week or more in the limited confines of a boat could be a struggle. My first trip to the Mergui Archipelago (aka The Burma Banks) was aboard a trimaran with accommodation for eight guests, but on this occasion there were only three of us.

Simon was the same age as me, but there the resemblance ended. A long-haired Californian, ex-hippy, ex-pot smoker, he had the obligatory ex-wife and dysfunctional family of ex-delinquents who had graduated to being grown-up pot smokers, and even in some cases ex-pot smokers, with ex-wives too, as seems to be the habit in California. Just about every Californian I have met has an ex-something in his, or her, life story.

A product of the 1960s Flower-Power era, Simon wore a permanent vacant expression on his face. When asked even a simple question, it seemed to take a long time to get through to his brain, and an even longer time to process the question and formulate an answer.

Conversation was challenging and convoluted as you waited for an answer, which was often enigmatic and so late in coming you had moved on and forgotten what the question was. He had spent a few years in the US Navy during the Vietnam War.

Gaia

"Did you enjoy life in the navy?"

Silence. His blue eyes stared towards the horizon. He showed no obvious signs of having heard the question. I waited. Then he shook his head. I probed further.

"What did you not like about it?" Silence. Maybe he did not like talking about it. Perhaps I had touched on a sensitive area. I decided to move on, leave him to his thoughts, and started talking to someone else.

A moment or two later, in the middle of my conversation, he said, "I am from California." We all knew that already. I looked at him in puzzlement...Another long pause, then he explained. "They are always telling you to do things in the navy. In California, we don't like to be told what to do."

He brought with him a laconic sense of humour, and a bowel-plugging dose of constipation that required some drastic medication from the ship's first aid kit to get his tubes cleared.

Melissa was a fifty-year old nurse from the USA, the single mother of a 33 year-old heroin addict. Another ex-pot smoker, she was now deep into Zen Buddhism and meditation. Paranoia was her hobby. She told me she dosed up on a variety of antibiotics before she arrived, just in case there might be some nasty bug waiting to attack her when she stepped off the plane. If it did, it would soon find out that she had the stuff within her to annihilate it, whatever it might be.

One night at around 2 a.m., she was aroused by the sound of a Myanmar fishing boat anchoring nearby. Paranoia kicked in. She imagined they were pirates coming to kill us all and steal our boat, so she locked herself in her cabin and sat on her meditation cushion for two hours until she was able to convince herself that they were not intent on murder and mayhem.

She also had the notion that these islands (nearly all uninhabited) may be infested with ruthless drug producers who would take exception to our vessel anchoring in their sheltered bays, and shoot us. Maybe she had been influenced by Alex Garland's novel, The Beach, or had seen the film based on the book. It was difficult to persuade her that this was highly unlikely.

Every fishing boat was regarded with deep suspicion. She was convinced that they were all rogues intent on serious mischief and begged our captain not to go near them when he went alongside one to buy some fish. When he brushed her paranoia aside, she said, "But they all look so dark and sinister. Maybe they just want us to think they're fishermen to lull us into a false sense of security." They were friendly and gave us some squid to feast on, but that did not satisfy Melissa. "Maybe it has been poisoned," she cautioned. You can only take so much of this and I suggested that her mind had been been corrupted by Hollywood movies, or writers with lurid imaginations. As with Simon's constipation, she could have benefitted from a dose of some purgative of the mind to cleanse her of all these weird notions.

Despite her incessant fears, she was well travelled, and had decided to take up diving. She had completed the theory part of the course, but had never been in the sea, so it was arranged that she could do the practical part of the course during this cruise, enabling her to become certified by the end of the week... Maybe.

Josh, our guide, was a certified dive instructor from San Francisco. He had rebelled against just about everything as he grew up (well, what else would you expect? He too was from California, so that seems quite normal). He established his own trucking business, made a heap of money, and sold out before the government suspected he may not be paying enough in taxes. He elected to travel and work abroad as a snowboard instructor in Japan, and a dive guide and instructor in South East Asia in the six months of each year when there is no snow in Japan. He had also taught English in Japan, and in the United Arab Emirates. Another ex pot-smoker (Well, what do you expect? He was from California), he was a thoughtful guy who hated so much of the hypocrisy in American politics and lifestyle today. I liked him.

And there was me, the real oddball of the group, who has never smoked pot, doesn't have an ex-wife (but a deceased one after 29 years of marriage – not many last that long in California), and never had delinquent children, or if they were, it was well concealed. I never got into trouble with the police, or the government for tax evasion, never got into meditation and Buddhism, nor any other fashionable 'ism.' I seemed so dull. The others looked at me in disbelief. "But how did you manage to avoid getting into all these things? Everybody does it."

Kawthung

"I don't come from California!" I retorted. "Let's just say I am a bit of a rebel, but one who rebelled against all the self-destructive things the self-styled rebels did to let it be known that they were rebels. It seemed stupid to me to poison a healthy body with drugs, or smoking cigarettes. Why? Because everyone else was doing it? Well, I can assure you, all the rest of the world is not the same as California. And as long as I am not doing it, and there are many others like me, it is fallacious to claim that *everyone* is doing it. You have a choice in who you imitate." Despite being an alien, I got on well with all of them.

My foray into Burmese waters began with a four-hour journey by road from Phuket to Ranong, a town on the river estuary that is the border between Thailand and Myanmar (formerly called Burma). A small boat took us across the estuary to Kawthaung on the Burmese side, where we had to deposit our passports with the immigration office and take on board a government official for the duration of our voyage. Every foreign boat seeking permission to sail in these waters must have a government official on board, feed him, and pay his wages. It is claimed that this is to ensure our safety in these waters, but from what or whom, no one is prepared to say. It seems like a good job-creation scheme – or vacation– for Burmese officials.

Jojo, our official, was a graduate in physics. His wife was a teacher, but he was making a better living cruising on the dive boats that work this area. He worked on board, helping us kit up for our dives, hauling the anchor, washing dishes, making tea. He was a real asset, a nice guy.

Having completed all the formalities, the immigration officers left our boat and we were able to leave the bustling harbour of Kawthaung, where long-tailed boats growled to and fro, bringing home fishermen, transporting catches of squid, taking people across the border to Thailand, or bringing them back to Myanmar.

We made passage towards the islands as the sun set. Delicious smells wafted up from the galley where the captain's Thai wife, an excellent cook, prepared our dinner. Despite having only two gas burners on her stove, she prepared the most delicious and varied dishes for every meal, offering both western and Thai food. The crew consisted of the captain, his wife, and one deckhand. Jojo helped out, turning his hand to any task required. As soon as I appeared from my cabin in the morning, one of them was by my side with a big smile, thrusting a mug of tea into my hand.

This cruise, a mixture of diving, sailing, kayaking, and scrambling through dense jungle, was fun – well, most of the time. The jungle was difficult. Traversing an island from one side to the other meant forcing a way through dense undergrowth, scrambling up steep, rocky, overgrown slopes on one side, and down steep rocky, overgrown slopes on the other. Plants here conspire to trap you. Creepers and vines ensnare you in their tendrils. They have an almost animal-like tendency to wrap themselves around your legs and ankles. Like wrestling with an octopus, you free yourself from one tendril only to discover that, while you were unraveling it, the others have wrapped you in an intimate embrace.

Some plants have long curving leaves armoured with stinging barbs along each edge that lock into your skin, hooking you in dozens of places. Others sport penetrating thorns that rip your legs to shreds. Large spiders' webs shimmer in the dappled sunlight, sometimes. At other times you stumble into them, clawing their sticky webs off your face, and look around for the spider. Where were the large spiders that made the webs? Were they lurking behind a branch of the tree waiting to leap on you and sink their fangs into the back of your neck? Maybe Melissa's paranoias were justifiable here! The mosquitoes whined and pined for your blood, and the sand flies danced a celebratory greeting for you on the beach: "Hey guys, we have some visitors for dinner tonight!" And they attacked our ankles with needle-sharp bites. At the end of this skin-ripping, shirt-tearing, ankle-biting, neck-slapping experience, you arrive at another white beach identical to the one you left – and then you have to endure the return journey as you curse your way back through the jungle. It's easy to understand why no one lives on such islands. The Moken sea gypsies have the right idea. They stay on their boats. No, the jungle here wasn't much fun.

We cruised in kayaks into idyllic turquoise-coloured bays fringed with white sand, and probed inlets and caves. You can get into nooks and crannies that only a small craft like a kayak can ever get into, where the only sound is the gentle lap of the waves and the scuttling of crabs scurrying along the rock faces. The landscape was pleasant and interesting to look at, but it was the sea, and in particular under the sea, that was fascinating and thrilling.

Almost every dive had its excitement; giant stingrays up to 2 metres across demonstrated the sinusoidal movement of their wings in elegant flight; cuttlefish seemed to doze with sleepy looking eyes; sleek, cold-eyed sharks patrolled the reefs; and there were caves, with who-knows-what lurking in their dark shadows.

Hordes of small dancer shrimps populated narrow fissures, like ballet dancers dancing around on tip-toe. Cleaner shrimps waved their white feelers at you from tight holes. Lay a hand on the rock and they will come out and pick away at your fingernails, cleaning them of the accumulation of dead cells where fingernail and skin meet. Many of the larger fish use them for cleaning and can often be seen having their bodies picked clean of parasites in the 'cleaning stations.' For every environment there was an animal with a purpose suited to it.

At night, the sea flashed like diamonds, the bioluminescence caused by dinoflagellates, tiny planktonic creatures agitated by any movement such as a passing fish or the anchor chain of the boat. One night it was particularly spectacular and Josh suggested we put on masks and snorkels and try a swim. Our hands stirred up a glow, like a million diamonds sparkling, as we thrust ourselves through the water. Watching another body swimming was like watching some ghostly creature glowing in the blackness of the sea. You couldn't see any of the features of the body, only the glow the bioluminescence created, ghost-like and eerie.

Simon had to take time to ponder (as usual) whether he would take the plunge. After a few moments of silent deliberation he said, "Okay, I'll go in." He stood up, took a step backwards, and did just that, falling off the stern into the sea, fully clothed. He'd forgotten the boat ended there. We were doubled up with laughter.

One small island, shaped like a bun, provided the highlight of the trip. On the north side, it offered a narrow canyon to explore. At the closed end of the canyon there were two features of interest; a dark hole like a mineshaft, and a large swim-through where a huge boulder had toppled against the island. Josh stopped, poked his head down into the dark hole, shone his torch around, but came up again shaking his head. Melissa, being a novice, was neither ready nor willing to try such an exploration, so Josh took us through the swim-through instead. I was disappointed. I wanted to see inside that black hole.

"I'd love to do that dive again," I said to Josh as we bobbed about in the sea, waiting for the boat to pick us up.

"We'll go down again before lunch, but without Melissa this time. She's not ready for this yet. And we can explore the cave."

She had found it all a bit overwhelming, so that was okay with her. Josh, Simon, and I dropped into the water again before mid-day and approached the cave from the opposite end. Josh handed me the torch and indicated for me to lead. He wanted to take photos and needed two hands to operate the camera. I kicked down into the gloom. A pillar of rock split the entrance tunnel into two channels. The cave was low, offering little more than a metre of headroom. The left side looked lower, so I took the right-hand route and shone the torch up ahead. I was close to the right-hand wall when the thick pillar ended, revealing a wider chamber to my left side. As I swung the torch round, examining walls and roof for marine life I noticed a large fin, almost touching the roof. "That's a shark's tail fin," I thought at once. "A big tail fin. There must be a big shark attached to it." I let the torch beam follow the line of the fin and traversed the length of the monster. But it wasn't a shark – it was two sharks, about three metres in length, lying side by side on the floor of the cave.

Two Nurse Sharks lying side by side

I flashed the torch back to the others, and then pointed the beam on to the sharks. Josh wasted no time and took some photos. The sharks were unimpressed by us, the only sign of life being the movement of their gills. I moved on into the darkness of the cave and saw a bluish hue up ahead, the light coming down the mineshaft-like hole at the north end. I powered my way towards it and inhaled to increase buoyancy. This elevated me up the shaft and out into the open sea.

Back on board for lunch, Josh said, "The plan for the afternoon is to go to another island for kayaking among the mangroves...." He looked at me. I could swear he was reading my mind. "Unless you want to dive here again."

"Definitely!" I said. Josh smiled.

"I thought you might feel that way, John." He then asked how the others felt. He offered to take Melissa on an easier dive to let Simon and I explore the depths again. As usual, Simon looked vague and pondered awhile. He then murmured, "Yeah, that's cool."

That afternoon we went down for the third time, rolling off the boat at the north end of the island. I was leading, heading for the cave to enter through the dark hole like a mineshaft. As we approached the opening, a great blotchy black sheet appeared out of the hole, a giant stingray. I veered off to the side and watched it glide away from me. I approached the entrance to the cave and started to descend head first, but Simon grabbed my fins and tugged. I looked round and he gave me the 'something's wrong' sign with his hand and pointed. The giant stingray was coming back. If the two sharks were still in there and we joined them, and a giant stingray almost two metres across tried to squeeze in there as well, it might become a wee bit too crowded – and there might be other stingrays in there already. We had seen four of them resting together that morning outside the south entrance.

But when it saw me emerge, it sheered off and glided down to rest on the sandy bottom of the gully. I plunged into the hole again to check things out. Simon hovered outside. I had a look around and then flashed the light up, gave him the OK signal, and he dropped in behind me.

The sharks were still there, but the current was stronger and they were having to move those massive bodies and tail fins to maintain their positions, making them even more awesome looking. Think of two big-bodied sharks, writhing in a snake-like motion. That gave us less room to pass them. If they panicked, and that tail lashed out sideways, it would give me the kind of slap my mother often administered to 'that boy!' I kicked forward and glided past them. Simon didn't hang about either. This was no place for a laid-back Californian to linger.

We circled the complete island, breaking the surface almost beside the boat. "Well done. Your navigation is spot on," cried Josh as he reached down to help us get back aboard.

Now just in case you think I am crazy having sharks as bed-fellows, these were nurse sharks, bottom feeders that eat small shrimps and crab – and I don't look much like either of these – so they were not likely to be tempted to taste me. Of course, I didn't know what they were until I was right in bed beside them. Nurse sharks have been known to sit still and let divers caress them. I read that in a book. But then I also read that they are ranked fourth in order of sharks known to have bitten humans, usually snapping at silly divers who become too intimate with them.

But that was after I got back ashore.

Chapter 28

A REAL MAN

My second exploration of Burmese waters was on Colona II, a 67 foot ketch. With a fresh offshore breeze filling her sails, I felt that indescribable feeling of fulfilment, satisfying a longing for the sea and sailing. There is something magical about sailing westwards. In my childhood, the sea lay to the west, the horizon to the west, adventure and the unknown all seemed to lie to the west, and I tingled with anticipation of what was to come on this new voyage to these remote islands.

Getting away from land always brings a feeling of relief to a mariner, a feeling of oneness with the sea and the boat. Colona II had sailed round the world in 1979 and had been on charter for diving in the Red Sea before coming to Thailand in the 1990s. Her Norwegian skipper and owner, Freddy Storheil, had based himself in Thailand after an adventurous life of sailing and diving in various parts of the world. Like many other European ex-pats, he had no wish to return to his homeland and the raw chill of a Norwegian winter.

His crew consisted of two local deckhands who did the cooking and everything else, the obligatory Burmese government official who helped out with on-board duties, and his old friend and guest for this voyage, Haakon Hellner, nicknamed Hawk. Hawk was a former Norwegian Air Force fighter pilot who became a commercial airline pilot flying Jumbo jets, until he retired the year before. Hawk and I were the same age, Freddy a couple of years younger. Roger Talbot from Newcastle, England, was our dive guide.

Colona II

Colona II can carry six divers. On this trip there were only three: myself, a 61 year-old English lady called Sue, and Tom, her 60 year-old American boyfriend. Sue was a competent and experienced diver, but Tom had not dived for many years. He was overweight and sucked twice as much air as the rest of us. That made all his dives short. Roger had to surface with Tom to ensure his safety, so Sue and I became a buddy team. She was a good buddy, and searched for photo opportunities for me. The others went off to their cabins around 9 p.m., but Hawk and I sat on deck, swapping yarns. Having flown to most parts of the world, he had a host of stories and proved to be an interesting shipmate.

This area is remote. There is not even a road connecting Kawthaung to the rest of Myanmar. Only a few dive boats come here from Thailand, so the dive sites were in excellent condition. Every night, fishermen from Myanmar and Thailand light up the night sky with powerful lanterns that attract squid to the surface, and to their doom.

These islands are home to the Moken people, a tribe of sea gypsies who meander among them in crude boats with only a simple roof slung across the boat for shelter.

Sea Gypsy boat

They're born on the sea, they live on the sea, they die on the sea. They know its moods. They're nomads, moving from island to island, living more than six months each year on their boats, only coming ashore to live in crude huts during the monsoon season. They collect sea cucumbers, catch eels and fish, dive for shellfish. They've been living this way for so many generations they've become almost amphibious. Their children learn to swim before they can walk. Underwater, their eyes have adapted. Without a mask, they can see much better than the rest of us, and by lowering their heart rate they can stay underwater for several minutes without any breathing apparatus. They do a little hand-line fishing, taking just enough to feed the family and to trade for fuel for their boats' engines. Despite their traditional way of life, they recognise the advantages of having a reliable diesel engine.

I felt privileged to be invited on board one of their boats, anchored for the night nearby. It was an open boat with a roof slung over the mid-section to provide shelter from both the heat of the sun and the rain. Fish were split and laid out on the roof to dry in the the sun, a simple way of preserving them. Inside this open-ended shelter, some pots and cooking utensils lined the narrow shelves, and they seemed to be the family's only household possessions. We brought them some fresh fruit. In return for our offering, we were accepted as friends, and allowed to take photographs.

At the forward end of the boat the eldest son, a boy of about 15, chopped a fish into chunks for some sort of stew, while his younger brother fished with a hand line from the bow. Another young brother and his sister sat watching mother and grandmother go about their tasks. Grandmother sat cross-legged on the hard boards, pounding something to a fine powder with mortar and pestle. The mother squatted on one side, tending a pot on a cooking fire contained within a metal bucket pierced with holes which sat on a flat stone. The smoke made its exit through the open ends of the shelter. While the women prepared dinner, the father greeted his visitors.

They speak no English. Many of them don't even speak Burmese, but our Burmese official was able to converse with them in their own language. In common with other vagrant peoples, the Moken are regarded as of lower status by the rest of Burmese society. They are mainly unschooled in a formal sense, but they know how to survive in this wilderness. They know how to build and maintain boats, to find food on land, in the sea, on the shores, and what herbs to gather for their medicinal properties.

It was their intimate knowledge of the sea that saved many of the Moken people from the devastation that affected other coastal communities on 26 Dec 2004 when the tsunami struck. Before the tidal wave bore down on their villages, the Moken people observed the peculiar behaviour of the sea as it drained from the shore to feed the wave. They moved to higher ground, avoiding loss of life, but their fragile dwellings were smashed to pieces.

They don't ask for handouts from the government. Attempts by both the Thai and Burmese governments to encourage them to adopt a more conventional lifestyle have met with only partial success. However, as in most other places, the traditional way of life is being eroded and their numbers are reported to be dwindling, though how anyone can tell is a mystery. These people are here today, gone tomorrow. Registering births and deaths is not part of their lifestyle. They don't need governing.

The downside of living in remote areas is that, if there is an accident, you are a long way from any assistance. There is no coastguard, no lifeboat service, no rescue helicopters to whisk a casualty off to hospital. For divers with decompression sickness, the nearest hyperbaric chamber is at Phuket. That means a lengthy sea passage to Myanmar, clear immigration, a cross-border boat ride to Thailand, more immigration procedures, and a 5-hour car drive to Phuket: not ideal if you have a life-threatening condition.

That scenario, which was spelled out in our briefing at the start of the voyage, had to be enacted on the second last day. After our third dive that day, Tom became ill. His body began to tingle and became blotched with blue marbled streaks all over it. Tom thought he was having a heart attack, but Freddy took one look and said, "Decompression sickness. We have to get him to hospital."

He was sent to his bunk and given oxygen. We set course for the mainland. By mid-night we had him in Thailand again, in a hired car to Phuket, arriving there around 5 a.m., about 12 hours after he first felt ill. There was no obvious reason for his sickness, but the doctor at the hyperbaric chamber remarked that most cases he sees are divers who are overweight. That brought the voyage to a premature end on a sad note.

It wasn't the only problem we'd encountered. The masthead navigation light, a tri-coloured light showing green and red forward to indicate starboard and port sides of the vessel, and a white light showing aft, had come adrift in rough weather. The fitting had been corroded over the years by the salt-laden air, and the light had toppled off the masthead and was dangling by the wires. This meant that the white light, which should only be visible from astern, was now showing forward, and the port and starboard lights were the wrong way round and showing aft, but these positions could change with the light dangling as the boat rocked in the waves.

It had to be fixed, but the top of the mast was 75 feet above the deck. The two deckhands and the Burmese official refused to climb the mast. Freddy was not prepared to do it himself. The last time he had done it, 10 years before, he was shaking all over and had to go to bed for the rest of the day to recover. Hawk, who was there as Freddy's guest, sat on deck drinking beer most days, so it was out of the question for him to attempt it. Roger, the dive guide, was a big fellow, six feet three, and would go up if it was absolutely necessary, but he had never been up a mast before and was not at all happy about it. Tom? Out of the question. Overweight, even climbing the steps out of the cabin left him gasping. Sue? She was in reasonable shape, but climbing 75 feet up a mast can be a stern physical test, as well as a mental challenge, and it did not seem an appropriate task for an imperious, 61 year-old English lady when there were seven men aboard. She hadn't a clue about what was likely to be involved in fixing the lights, nor was she at all keen on the idea. How could the men have held up their heads if she had been the only one willing to do it? I offered to go up.

"Oh, no John. You are too old. It is too dangerous," said Freddy.

I growled at him. "Freddy, I've been up and down my own mast dozens of times. And I've been up other people's masts, fixing things for them. It'll be no problem." As everyone in his crew had mutinied, I reckoned one more would not make any difference. I hopped up on the boom and shot up the mask to assess the situation, came back down and told Freddy what I needed for repairs, climbed back up, and ten minutes later the lights were fixed. Freddy was delighted and pumped my hand. "John, from now on your drinks are free!"

Hawk was there already by my side, with a glass in his hand for me. "John, you went up that mast like a monkey, not once, but twice, and so effortlessly! Sit down and let me pour you a rum and coke. You deserve it."

It felt good to be useful, and I had a great view of the boat from 75 feet above the deck. The two deckhands always seemed to assume that at my age I needed their help to get in and out of the water, but 'Mr John' had won their respect after that.

As always, the imperious Sue had the last caustic word.

"Thank goodness there is one *real* man on board this vessel."

Chapter 29

MALDIVES

The Maldives consist of two parallel lines of coral atolls, lying in a north to south formation to the south of India. For many, it is the ideal tropical island paradise. You can fly in to the resorts by seaplane from Male International Airport and have your luggage carried from the plane to your room. You can eat, sleep, lounge around the pool, or swim till your holiday is over. Idyllic, if you like that kind of thing, but I am not comfortable lazing around, being pampered. I prefer activity.

Male, the capital, is not idyllic. A small city, it occupies the entire island, about 3 km long and 2 km wide, with narrow congested streets. It has no merit, as far as I could see. Tourists usually head straight to the luxury island resorts. The International Airport is situated on a neighbouring island, and small ferries shuttle back and forth between the airport and Male, day and night, a 15-minute trip. I had a walk around Male's streets on my overnight stay before embarking on the MV Stingray. Cafes and restaurants were filled with men. Wives or girlfriends were nowhere to be seen. In this Moslem state, the women seem to be confined to the home while the men go out to relax, drink coffee (alcohol is forbidden), and socialise. It was a relief next morning to board Stingray.

Stingray at anchor

A comfortable, live-aboard dive boat, Stingray can accommodate 18 divers in shared cabins, but with only 14 aboard, I had a cabin to myself. A helpful crew and a sociable bunch of divers from Austria, Denmark, France, Italy, and the USA, contributed to a pleasant social and diving experience. With a good on-board atmosphere, we had a rollicking New Year's Eve party.

The Maldives claims to be a great place to see manta rays and whale sharks. Well, the mantas were pretty shy when I was there, only making an appearance at one site. After clinging to the rocks on the bottom for the whole dive, waiting in a strong current until we had run out of bottom time, we managed a brief glimpse of a couple on the way up, but they were just two fleeting shadows in the gloom. On Jan 1, the first dive of the year provided a passing whale shark, emerging like a submarine out of the gloom, but it was too far off to get a decent photo and it was unwilling to wait and pose for us.

Sharks abound; grey reef sharks, white-tips, silver tips, hammerheads too. As I was flying out at 1:30 a.m, I had to skip the last dive to complete my 24 hours no-fly time after diving, and that was when the hammerheads made their appearance. On one dive, a school of mobula rays came flying past like a formation of delta-winged aircraft. They resemble mantas in appearance, but are smaller. This is a location to suit those who like the large fish to be found in places with strong currents.

However, what the Maldives lacked for me was the unusual, the intriguing, the bizarre – the smaller stuff that I find absorbing. There must be plenty of it around, but the dive guides seemed only interested in offering sites where the big fish were to be seen. It is not difficult to find a shark on your own, but a pygmy seahorse, or a hairy frogfish, often requires a guide who knows where to look, and has the patience to find it. I saw nothing new until the last day. As we waited for the group to gather to surface at the end of a strong current dive, the guide noticed something odd in a hole in the reef. It was a kind of shrimp I had never seen before, nor had anyone else on board, including the guides. Checking the identification books it proved to be a marble shrimp, of the saron genus.

Saron shrimp

Although a very enjoyable and colourful dive trip, taking all things into consideration, especially cost, the Maldives would not entice me back. I am surprised that some divers return year after year when they could see much more in Indonesia or the Philippines for less cost. But the lure of the big fish is powerful. Mantas are always impressive and thrilling to see, and a whale shark is overwhelming because of its size, but sharks in general do not excite me. They are grey, distant, timorous, but they are sleek, efficient machines designed with such perfection they have hardly evolved at all in millions of years.

I prefer a range of colourful, interesting, and unusual animals to photograph: the intriguing small creatures of the oceans. I much prefer diving in the Philippines (much cheaper too) and in Indonesia, both of which have an extensive marine biodiversity.

The Maldives is orientated towards the high-spending tourist market: especially the honeymoon couples who want pampering on a tropical island. They also attract European and American divers who don't mind paying 300 US dollars per night for an overnight stay before embarking on a live-aboard. I travelled and dived for six months, and $300 rooms were not in my budget. I could do a lot of dives for $300. My in-bound arrival time left me no alternative but to seek accommodation at the cheap end of the market in Male. It cost $80 per night for a bed, with breakfast extra. In the Philippines, I could rent an apartment for just over $8 per night! I am a different class of traveller.

I saw a far greater diversity of marine life in Thailand, Indonesia, Papua, and the Philippines, for a fraction of the cost. As a photographer, your feelings about a dive are based on what you capture on camera, not just viewing the big scene and the big fish, which are often too far away and lacking in colour to get a really good photo. If I put aside my grouse about not seeing many small things, it was still an enjoyable experience. These tiny islands do have that paradise look about them, but even paradise can throw up some unpleasant surprises.

At the end of a drift dive between two submerged reefs, my buddy, a French lady called Magali, and I surfaced together and looked around in amazement. The sea had been flat calm on entering just over an hour before. It was now whipped into a frenzy of menacing, white breakers by a strong wind howling under a leaden sky. Worse than that, we could not see any sign of the dive boat! When you are all alone on the surface of a turbulent sea, with a strong tide sweeping you into the vast expanse of the Indian Ocean under a darkening sky, without an island or even a solitary palm tree in sight, you may feel entitled to a having a wee panic.

"Oh My God. They have gone away and left us!" cried out Magali.

"No. They must be around somewhere." I said, as we were tossed around in the turbulent tide race, but where?

The dhoni, the small boat that took us from Stingray, had dropped us off about half a mile away at the entrance to the channel between the two hidden reefs. All we had to do was keep the reef on our left side and we would drift along to the pick up area. I had been taking photos and Magali had been looking for things for me, and keeping an eye on which direction the others had gone. The reef, which had started as a fairly steep slope, had flattened out. We had found some interesting photo opportunities on this plateau and had drifted away from the others. The dive time had been set at around 60 minutes, so when our time was up we surfaced.

Maldives has many colourful reefs

The waves were at least a metre and a half high, and that was the problem. If we were in a trough, or the dhoni was in a trough some way off, neither could see the other.

Having experienced this before in the Coral Sea, I realised I must crest the waves at the same time as the dive boat, and sure enough there it was, about three hundred metres away, wallowing beam-on to the seas, as she hauled the last of the other divers aboard.

"There it is," I roared. "She'll come and pick us up."

While on our safety stop at 5 metres, I had inflated my surface marker buoy, a long, red sausage-like balloon to show the boat where we were. However, once the other divers were aboard the dhoni, it turned to head into the breaking seas and began to look for us where it thought we might surface. But we had travelled further in the current, and the boat was now heading away from us, the distance between us and the dhoni increasing with every passing second. What was disconcerting was that no one seemed to think of looking astern for us. And there was no sign of Stingray. It had moved on to shelter at our next anchorage.

"Oh John, they are leaving us behind!" cried out Magali as the boat headed away from us.

"No. Don't worry. They know we are not aboard. They will do a square search pattern and see us when they turn." I hoped my assurance would ease her fears, but dive boats have been known to lose divers. It has happened before, in Australia and Indonesia, and Philipp, my German buddy, with whom I dive each year, had a nightmare experience in the Philippines, when a group he was with spent 26 hours in the sea before being found by a fisherman.

I could see the newspaper headlines: Divers Missing in Shark Infested Waters – they love to dramatise it – but it was not an appealing thought. I grabbed my whistle and blew with all my might to attract their attention, and Magali cried out as loud as she could, but it was futile. The strengthening wind carried all sound away behind us. The boat receded into the distance, often remaining hidden in the troughs for what seemed an eternity before reappearing as we crested the waves simultaneously.

Then, as I had predicted, it turned broadside on to the waves and started the second leg of its search pattern. "They'll surely see us now," I cried, imagining the lookouts peering right and left as well as ahead, but why never astern? Then, as I crested a wave I saw her turn back towards us. "She's coming for us now," I called to Magali. She looked at me, ashen faced.

"Oh John, I was so afraid they were leaving us. I will never dive again."

"Och, don't be daft. You love diving. You can't give it up. It was only a matter of time till they turned and saw us. Besides, what will I do without my buddy? I need you with me down there to look after me. You are not giving up! We do the next dive – together!"

It's great what a wee bit of assertiveness can do. She smiled. The boat drew alongside, leaping and bucking in the waves. We passed our fins and tanks to the deckhand and climbed up the short ladder, not the easiest task with the boat bouncing up and down like a cork. I saw Magali up the ladder first, then clambered aboard.

"Are you OK, John?" asked the deckhand, helping me with a steady hand. I grinned. "Sure." Then I growled at him, "But I would have swallowed a lot less sea water shouting at you if you had kept a lookout astern!"

I wriggled out of my gear as he secured my air tank to the side of the vessel. He patted me on the shoulder and gave me a dazzling smile. "Ah, you're okay, John. You strong man."

As the dhoni punched through the waves and into a sheltered lagoon where Stingray lay with twin anchors out to hold her against the freshening wind, I reflected on how the crew had changed their attitude over the past few days. I was by far the oldest aboard, and on the first day or two they had been keen to help 'the old man' along with a steadying hand and words like, "Careful now, John," as I stepped from Stingray on to the dhoni. However, after a couple of days they noticed the old man was one of the last to emerge from the depths, and had more air left than most. I had earned some respect

And Magali did come with me on the next dive.

Chapter 30

PALAU

"Palau? Where is that?" Other than among the diving fraternity, no one I met in the Philippines, Palau's closest neighbour to the west, seemed to have heard of the place. I doubt if many others will have much knowledge of Palau either. A small island republic in the Pacific Ocean with a population of about 18,000 people, it lies about 600 miles east of the Philippines and is one of the top dive spots in the world. It is expensive to get to from other parts of the world, but I was already in the Philippines, so it only took about hour and a half by air to get me there from Manila. I also planned to dive at Yap and Truk Lagoon, in the neighbouring Federated States of Micronesia.

The indigenous people are stubborn in their attitude towards work. It is something to be done only when necessary. They work till they get paid, then take time off until lack of money to buy beer forces them to work again. Survival is not a problem. Food is abundant: go fishing, pick fruit and coconuts. Few Palauans work in the hotels, shops, and restaurants. They are nearly all staffed by Filipinos. A third of the population is Filipino, because they *will* work.

Koror, the main island, is a pleasant place with a wide, main thoroughfare and modern buildings. Tourism, the mainstay of the economy, is booming. Large hotels cater mainly for Japanese, Korean, and American customers, but a fair number of Europeans endure the long flights to get here for diving.

Despite its remoteness, two people recognised me within the first three days. On my first day there, an Italian diver approached me and said, "You were at Malapascua, in the Philippines, last year in October." Correct. Maximo was formerly the technical director of Lamborghini, the prestigious Italian sports car company. Now self-employed as an engineering design consultant, he enjoys more time for diving.

On my third day, I went into the internet café. A familiar face looked up from its computer and its eyes opened wide. It was Jason Shaw, whom I had met on the Stella Maris at Tubbataha Reef in the Philippines nine months earlier. A lawyer from the USA, he had landed a nice job in Palau as district prosecutor, with easy access to the excellent diving.

Who would have believed I would meet two people who knew me on such a tiny, remote island in the vastness of the Pacific Ocean? In fact, there were actually three who knew me. Jason told me that Paul, who had been our cruise director on the Tubbataha trip, was working on one of the live-aboard boats that cruise around Palau.

The few inhabited islands are so close together they are connected by bridges. The others, hundreds of them, are the remnants of ancient reefs formed millions of years ago that have been thrust above the surface of the ocean. They present a remarkable landscape; steep-sided pinnacles with dense green foliage, white sandy bays, pale turquoise water over the shallow reefs, and dark green to dark blue in the deep channels.

Currents are strong, supplying nutrients from deep in the ocean, and that attracts big fish. Sharks are everywhere. Blue Corner is good spot to watch them. Drop your reef hook to anchor yourself in the current, and the sharks come out of the blue; prowling around, their sleek, streamlined forms glide through the water. Accustomed to divers, they mingled among us as we hovered motionless. Cameras clicked, and video cameras followed their graceful movements.

Some large Napoleon Wrasse were curious enough to have a close look at us. They have such friendly faces. One enjoyed being stroked. But touching anything underwater can be a risky business for the diver who may suffer stings, cuts, or abrasions, or for the fish, which may suffer skin disease through contact with us.

A Japanese wartime shipwreck provided some poignant images. A freighter, it had been carrying depth charges, now lying around in an untidy pile in one of the holds. Motor vehicle engines were stored in another. Around the stern-mounted gun, ripped off its mountings and now lying askew, lay canisters loaded with shells it never had time to fire. A rifle, heavily encrusted with growths, and a large saucepan with a gas mask inside, had been placed in an open spot so that divers could see them without having to penetrate the dark chambers that once were occupied by men. It was a poignant reminder of the horrors of war.

The Blue Hole, one of the world's best-known dive sites is a big hole in the reef. Down this large funnel, lies a cathedral-like chamber at 20 to 30 metres depth. Openings on the sides allow light in, each one creating a pale blue glow that illuminates the cavern. The walls are clothed in marine growths and its crevices contained some electric clams. It never fails to thrill to see that electric-blue lightning flash across this bi-valved shellfish's open mouth. It seems to say "Keep Off."

At the bottom of the Blue Hole, a tunnel leads you into a cavern called the Temple of Doom. Its narrow entrance allows only one diver at a time to go through, but once inside, the chamber is enormous. And dark. A white rope has been stretched across this cavern as a guide. Follow that, and your torchlight reveals the skeletons of some turtles that had wandered in here and could not find their way out, hence the name, Temple of Doom. Total blackness can be very disorienting. I usually have a good sense of direction, but in there, with no terms of reference, it had me confused after I stopped to photograph some shrimps I spotted on the floor of the cave.

However, as I was about to press the shutter, the female half of our pair of 'divers from hell' (a Russian couple) came barging into me with her enormous camera. The shrimps took off into the darkness, and her fins stirred up clouds of white dust. She was an absolute disaster.

Her partner was not much better. They had no awareness of their surroundings, and often barged into other divers. They finned as if they were in a sprint, and left a trail of broken pieces of coral. And her buoyancy control! She left me speechless.

I had watched in amusement when she had been raised by a strong current while we were hooked on to watch the sharks at Blue Corner. She dumped air to get back down, but never thought to re-inflate to stop her descent. Dropping like a bomb, she landed on a group of divers who were hooked on, watching the sharks. She, and her huge camera and its gantry with lights, became entangled with the divers below. From the mess of arms and legs, photographic equipment, and air hoses, the divers tried to extricate themselves. One turned on to his back to try to free himself and found her sitting astride him, with her crotch in his face and her legs tangled in his air hose, as they wrestled with each other to free themselves.

I don't understand what it is about Russians. Poor training? No common sense? Or just a devil-may-care, selfish attitude? In Komodo, the dive boat I was on refused to take bookings from Russians. In Sipadan, I heard horror stories about their lunatic behaviour, when two lives were lost through sheer stupidity, going deep, never to return. I had seen the same dangerous behaviour at Moalboal in the Philippines, from a Russian who was banned forever from diving at that resort.

Chandelier Cave has a chamber known as the Crocodile's Bedroom. The only way in and out is by diving. And how does a crocodile get in and out of its bedroom? That's right, it has to dive too, using the same tunnel as we did. That's a sobering thought. Once we were all in there, our guide showed us the ledge in a small cave to the side of the chamber where the crocodile liked to sleep. However, it hadn't been seen for some time. "No one has ever been attacked by it," he said, "Palauan crocodiles are tourist-friendly."

This cavern had four chambers, each with an air pocket where you can surface in the chamber and gaze at the sight revealed by your torchlight. It is similar to a huge cathedral with ornately carved walls.

Jellyfish lake is another peculiarity. One of several inland lakes, it was formed around 15,000 years ago. The islands at that time began to slip into the sea, and what had been a valley above sea level in the middle of the island became flooded as the sea made its way through fissures in the limestone. The result was a salt water lake, fed by the sea as the tides rise and fall. It became home to a couple of species of jellyfish that have remained there ever since. Featured in National Geographic Magazine in the 1982, it has become a major tourist attraction. Like the Palau crocodiles, the jellyfish are also tourist-friendly and do not sting you. You are only allowed to snorkel here. Diving is forbidden as toxic hydrogen sulphide gas is produced in the deep silt on the lake bottom by organic matter decaying. Stirring this layer up with fins would release the gases and kill the jellyfish.

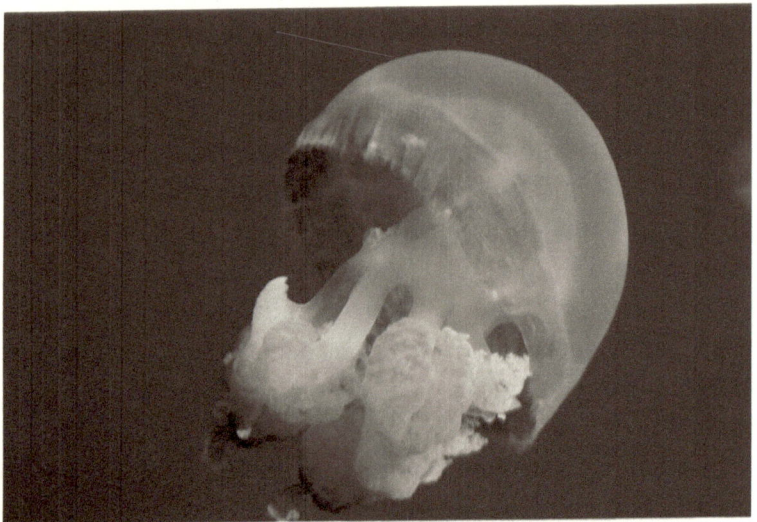

In Jellyfish lake

Snorkelling is sufficient to enjoy this unique experience. When you hover in that warm water in the soft light of the afternoon sun, watching the rhythmic pulsating of thousands of these beautiful animals around you, it is impossible not to feel an intense tranquility. They brush against your body, caressing you, inducing a sense of euphoria. It is a dream-like experience in which time and the world outside lose all meaning.

It would be excellent therapy for people suffering from stress.

Chapter 31
YAP

O nly six passengers got off the plane at Yap, making baggage collection and immigration clearance quick and easy. The immigration officer was polite and friendly and wished me a happy stay on Yap. A Yapanese warrior in traditional dress greeted us with a warm welcome and draped flowery garlands over our shoulders, a nice touch, which alleviated the discomfort of arrival at 3:15 a.m. I began to think this was a place that might rival the friendliness of the Cook Islands, but it went downhill from then on.

The people I met here were more laid back than in any other island group I have encountered in the Pacific, but laid back to the point of being immobile. How long does it take to cook a fried egg and a couple of strips of bacon? Five minutes maybe? Not on Yap. They need half an hour. There is no point in getting flustered. Action is anathema to them. It is easier to shrug and accept their way of life. Relax. Of course, but...

The frustrations build up. I had booked a dive and accommodation package several months earlier, and supplied my credit card details for final payment depending on the number of dives I did. Meanwhile, the owner of the business had died in a diving incident, and no one

195

else knew what business he had completed. He was the only signatory to the bank account, which had been frozen since his death, and the dive business could not use its credit card machine. They told me to pay in cash. I didn't have enough cash. I went to the Bank of the Federated States of Micronesia, the only bank on the island, to draw cash from my UK account using my bank card. Simple? Not so.

There is no cash machine in this entire state, and if you don't have a bank account in this bank, you can't withdraw money over the counter. Yap still hasn't found its way into the 20th century, let alone the 21st.

After some negotiations, the hotel allowed me to include the cost of the diving when paying my bill by credit card. They would then pass on the relevant amount, in cash, to the dive shop. But they charged me 7% extra for this service. Add to that the 2.5% service charge my own bank levied for a foreign currency transaction and I was paying nearly 10% more. All because the owner of the dive shop had no common sense and gone on a deep dive to please a stupid American woman who wanted to go deep (87 metres, 284 feet, according to their dive computers), on a single tank of air. That's more than twice the depth limit for air diving. She survived after treatment in a hyperbaric chamber. He did not. I had been offered a 10 % discount for making the booking four months early and agreeing to pay by credit card. Now I was being charged the full rate and had to stump up 10% extra as a result of his stupidity.

As it was the owner's negligence that led to this situation, I saw no reason why I should be penalised by having to pay more. I was only prepared to pay the agreed price. I had fitted in some extra diving for which I would be charged. Fair enough. I suggested a compromise. I would pay the hotel the package price by credit card and they could give the cash for diving to the dive shop for which I would be charged 7% extra, but the dive shop could compensate me for that extra cost by allowing me to have the extra diving free of charge. The stalemate was resolved. Travelling to remote places can be challenging!

Yap was a massive disappointment. In what claims to be the number one location for seeing manta rays in the world, only one manta was sighted in its murky waters. Visibility was poor throughout my stay. That was just bad luck. On another day it could have been clear with maybe a dozen mantas. But what really disappointed me was the state of the coral. Much of it was dead.

Early Yap currency – it has not progressed much

On the last day, the weather improved and we were able to dive the exposed outer reefs to the south of the island, which the guide said had the best dive sites. One wall dive was average with some life on it, but the rest was a sad picture of what is happening in so many parts of the world. Over 60% of the coral reefs are dead.

Sea temperatures have increased high enough to kill a lot of the coral. Is it our fault, creating climate change by our lifestyle? Or is it a natural phenomenon? The debate rages on. Whatever the reason, Yap presented a depressing picture compared to the excellent dive sites I had seen in South East Asia, or even neighbouring Palau.

The cost of everything was high, as is to be expected on a remote island, but the cost/quality relationship did not balance out. I paid high prices for mediocre food and poor service. Compared with Palau where you can have good quality, freshly prepared Thai, Indian,

Chinese, Korean, Japanese or western style food, this place fell far short in the catering sphere.

The waitresses in general were sullen, chewing betel nut and tobacco, so they could hardly speak. From time to time, they spat out a mouthful of scarlet juice into a bin in a corner of the restaurant. What does that do for ambience? They had no interest in their work, unlike the charming Filipinas who served in the restaurants at Palau.

You have to watch where you tread as the islanders are forever chewing betel nuts and tobacco, spitting out mouthfuls of the blood-red juice on the streets. Their teeth are stained with the red and brown dyes of the nuts and the tobacco, with the teeth slowly rotting away under the onslaught of chemicals in the juice. It looks hideous.

At the airport on my departure, I was greeted with the utmost courtesy by the staff, as they had been on my arrival; so different from those dull, dumpy, betel nut chewing waitresses who served in the restaurants. The immigration officer told me he hoped I would come back, but I hadn't the heart to tell him, "No way."

After checking in my baggage, I had time to kill as I waited for the incoming flight. Two guys sitting on a verandah at a café beside the terminal were playing guitars and singing. I wandered over. They were good. I pulled out the spoons and joined them.

"Hey, that's cool, man! We should have had you join us when we were playing at the hotel last night," said one. Later in the departure lounge, an American who'd been listening opened up a conversation about them as well. He too had been fascinated.

Play spoons, and make friends. It was the best part of my stay on Yap.

Chapter 32

TRUK LAGOON

Chuuk, one of the Federated States of Micronesia, is a group of 15 small islands surrounded by a near-circular 140-mile barrier reef that encloses one of the largest atoll lagoons in the Pacific Ocean – Truk Lagoon. Around 200 smaller atolls lie beyond the reef. Most of Chuck's 50,000 inhabitants live on the five largest islands, grouped together in the centre of the lagoon. The outer reef marks the edge of the vast caldera of this ancient volcano, beyond which its slopes tumble for around 3000 metres (almost 10,000 feet) to the cold, dark floor of the Pacific Ocean.

Linguistic and archaeological evidence suggests that the first settlers in the islands of Micronesia arrived over 2000 years ago, migrating across the Pacific Ocean from South East Asia. It is believed Chuuk was first populated around 1400CE from neighbouring Kosrae. The first Europeans arrived in 1526, when the Spanish claimed sovereignty and ruled the islands until 1899, when Spain sold its holdings to Germany. The Germans allegedly had difficulty pronouncing Chuuk, and it became known to them as Truk Lagoon. They were not popular overlords and, after a rebellious uprising in 1910-11, control of the islands passed to Japan in 1914. The Japanese brought development and prosperity to the islands – and the most terrifying event in its history.

Truk Lagoon's sheltered waters became the Japanese Imperial Fleet's Central Pacific forward base in World War II, from which supplies were distributed to warships and submarines operating far from their home bases.

At dawn on 17 February 1944, the drone of 450 American bombers was the prelude to a devastating blow to the Japanese war effort in the Pacific. Wave after wave of American bombers brought terror and destruction on a vast scale. Japanese aircraft were scrambled to its defence, but 37 were destroyed before they could leave the ground. The attack continued on 18 February and met with little resistance as the islands' anti-aircraft defences had been destroyed by bombing the previous day, and the airfield runway had been left full of bomb craters. With air defences immobilised, the bombers picked off ship after ship, sinking them with bombs and torpedoes launched from low-flying aircraft.

In two days, over 400 Japanese aircraft were rendered useless and more than 50 ships were sunk. Japanese casualties numbered over 600, Americans less than 30. Only 22 US aircraft were lost, and 28 US airmen were picked up from the sea by a patrolling submarine. The attack was a resounding success, restricting operations by Japanese naval forces in the Pacific. With supplies of food, fuel, medical supplies, and ammunition cut off, even the largest Japanese warships had to turn for home, unable to operate in distant waters.

Having dealt this killer blow, the US forces left Chuuk alone. While the US forces pressed on towards the Philippines and Japan, Chuuk was ignored for almost two years. Its people and the Japanese forces left there, starved of supplies from the outside world, had to revert to subsistence living. The sea provided plenty of fish, and coconuts and fruits were available in abundance on land.

Operation Hailstorm, as this attack was code-named, brought Chuuk to the attention of the diving fraternity in the 1960s, when exploration of the sunken ships of the Japanese supply fleet began. Many were almost intact, still with cargoes in their holds.

Arguably the best wreck diving location in the world, this museum of World War II naval history draws divers from all over the world to this lonely outpost in the middle of the Pacific. The ships at Chuuk have not been stripped of their valuable assets, such their bronze propellers. Engine rooms are often intact, with machinery clearly visible in the light of the diver's torch. Dark passageways can be navigated to toilets, galleys, cabins. Their holds still contain artillery shells, depth charges, tanks, trucks, fighter aircraft, and spare parts. A submarine supply ship carries torpedoes and spare warheads, extra periscopes to replace those damaged by depth charge attack, bottles of wine, cases of beer. It is an impressive display of the logistics of war.

Japanese tank

To swim through the enormous gap in a ship's side created by the explosive force of a torpedo, and view the destruction inside the ship is an awesome testament to the destructive forces unleashed here. These ships were the temporary homes of the men, ripped apart by horrific explosive force, terrifying noise, and fire.

The passageways, often littered with the debris of the blast of explosion, and the cargo holds of these dead ships still serve a purpose. They offer protection from large predators to vast numbers of small fish.

The external surfaces are now richly encrusted with marine algae, corals, anemones, sponges, and tube-worms. All the growths that you would expect to find on a natural reef are here, providing a new structure, an external skeleton, that will engulf the steel on which it is based, as the ever-expanding coral swallows up each ship. Already the masts, guns and derricks are thickly encrusted, their details now obscured, only their general outline informing the observer of their original function. Built by man, destroyed by man, these ships have now been recreated by nature into something of wondrous beauty.

Lurking in the shadows. Crown of Thorns Starfish

This powerful magnet for divers, so far from everywhere, is not an easy place to reach. But that unique historical record, of a chapter in the violence of a war that shook the world when I was a child, was irresistible. I had to see it for myself.

As a place to live, Chuuk leaves much to be desired. It was expensive. Most of the food and materials are imported from abroad; from Japan, China, or the United States. Its 'capital city,' on the island of Weno, is little more than a collection of rough huts, reminiscent of the gold-rush towns portrayed in old western movies. This is real wild-west territory too. The indigenous people have developed a liking for beer, often go crazy when drunk, and old tribal feuds erupt. Violence is a common way of settling disputes. The owner of our hotel told me one local fellow, driven by alcohol-fuelled rage, had taken a dislike to cars, and had chased them with a machete in hand. You may think a machete wielding maniac, in terms of speed, is no match for a car. But this is Chuuk, where the roads are so potholed they look like they have never been patched up since the American bombs dropped in 1944. No car was ever seen moving at more than 5 miles per hour: any faster would shake the car to pieces. And in these conditions, a machete wielding madman becomes a formidable threat.

Visitors were advised not to go out at night. But as one of my American dive buddies said, "Why would anyone want to go out at night here? There is nothing to see or do. There is nothing but shacks and shit here."

I went out to explore the town after diving one day and was met with smiles and friendly greetings. I never felt threatened – except by the enormous potholes in the road, filled with grey water of unknown depth. There were no pavements. Walking along a grass verge, and remember, this is the downtown area of the 'capital city,' I sank into soft mud that sucked the flip-flops off my feet. No one seemed to have thought of digging a small channel to let the water drain off the road into the sea, only a few feet way. But that would be work, a concept alien to the culture of Chuuk.

An American development aid worker told me: "Nothing works here. The roads are unspeakable. Piles of rubbish lie rotting by the roadside, or in heaps in back yards. Few homes have electricity, and the power supply is forever cutting out. The water system is a mess. Telecommunications are unreliable. There is no TV, not even radio!"

No radio? That's like going back to the earliest days of the 20th century in most other parts of the world. The hotel had a TV set in each room, but to see anything on it you had to hire DVD's, and even then you were at the mercy of Chuuk's temperamental power supply.

He went on: "There is no economy as such. The place is dependent on foreign aid. Most people 'work' for the government, which is a bit of a joke; it's just a glorified welfare system. They get paid for doing little or nothing – and doing it badly! Many of those who do work disappear for several days after pay-day, taking time off to relax and enjoy the money they have earned. That usually means getting drunk and beating up their neighbours.

"Corruption is rife. One of the supreme court judges was imprisoned after being found guilty of what was described as 'only a white-collar crime,' the misappropriation of government funds. And he had the temerity to demand that he should be released from prison on the days when the court was sitting, in order to preside over the trials of other criminals, and so continue to earn his salary."

Our hotel had an impressive menu that included several kinds of steaks, but when one of my American dive buddies ordered a T-bone steak, the waitress said, "We have no steaks. The ship has not arrived yet."

I ordered fish.

"We have no fish. The ship has not arrived yet."

And this is an island in the middle of the Pacific Ocean! But to catch a fish means doing something. And the Chuukies seem averse to doing anything, other than drinking beer. Strangely enough, there never seemed to be any shortage of beer! No doubt that formed the bulk of the cargo of 'The Ship.'

At breakfast, I ordered tea and toast with jam.

"We have no tea and no jam. The ship has not arrived yet."

I groaned.

"Would you like a drink, sir?"

"Yes, coca cola please."

"We have no cola."

And yes, you've guessed it. "The ship has not arrived yet."

The steaks, the fish, the tea, the jam, the cola, and the fuel for the electricity generator are delivered from the mainland. But that is the USA, several thousand miles across the ocean. A ship will only come this way if it has sufficient cargo to deliver, so you have to wait until it builds up enough freight to make a stop here worthwhile. Then you can have steak, fish, jam with your tea and toast, or a bottle of coca cola.

I didn't want to wait that long.

Life on Chuuk was a mixture of comedy and tragedy, but the diving was excellent.

Chapter 33

NEW AGE – OLD AGE

Computer keyboards, phones, micro-wave ovens, TV, cash machines, elevators: everything seems designed for finger-tip control in this push-button age. But some find it difficult to adapt. One such is my dive buddy, Mr-Ray-From-The-USA, whose face never fails to show signs of keyboard phobia when confronted with an array of buttons. Mobile phones rebel against him. Cash machines shut down in terror when he approaches. Elevators go on strike the moment he enters.

For some time he had been pestering me to take time off from diving to become a tourist. He likes company for travelling. He had only seen the airport at Bangkok and wanted to see some of the city's attractions, and visit Cambodia to see the temples of Angkor Wat. I relented when Philipp, our German dive buddy who was working in Dubai at that time, expressed an interest in joining us. I was glad of that. As always, Ray's amazement and curiosity at all he saw led to incessant chatter, so Philipp's ears acted as a firewall and gave me some respite from the continuous assault of sound from Ray (our friendship thrives on insults, by the way). He claims the following is a work of fiction, but I have Philipp as a witness.

Royal Palace, Bangkok

The Skytrain in Bangkok is an easy way to get around the city –
unless your name is Mr-Ray-From-The-USA. Press the button for
your destination on the ticket machine, put your money in the slot,
and the machine gives you a ticket. Philip did that for him to show
him how easy it was. Walk to the platform gate and slip your ticket
into the slot. It sucks it in and spits it out of another slot a few inches
ahead. Pick it up and the barrier opens. Walk through. Easy – unless
you are Mr-Ray-From-The-USA!

There are four ways of inserting a ticket: an arrow on the surface
shows you the correct way, but Mr Ray was very good at trying all the
wrong ways before he hit on the right one. He frowned as the machine
spat his ticket back out at him each time he inserted it. When it accepted
his ticket at the fourth attempt, he threw his arms up in the air, eyes wide
in amazement, and stepped forward to the barrier. It refused to open.

"What's wrong now?"

"Take your ticket out of the slot!"

He removed the ticket. The barrier opened. His arms went up in
the air in celebration again: "Hey, I got it!"

And the barrier snapped shut again.

"What did I do wrong now?"

"You stood there talking, instead of walking through!"

We found a station attendant who over-ruled the barrier and let Ray loose on the skytrain.

It took four trips before he managed to get in and out of the platforms without mishap. With a smug look on his face he proclaimed, "At last, I have joined the 21st century!"

"I wouldn't go quite that far, Ray!" I growled. He went to a cash machine to withdraw some money. It spat his card back out and would have nothing to do with him.

Our trip to Cambodia was delightful. Angkor Wat is complex of Buddhist and Hindu temples, as religious preferences varied, built over a period of around 300 years from the 12th century. Falling under Thai control after one of their wars with the Cambodians, the temples were abandoned and the jungle swallowed them up for around five hundred years. Re-discovered by the French during their colonial expansion in South East Asia in the middle of the 19th century, the temples have been designated a UNESCO World Heritage Site that attracts millions of people each year.

I had arranged a car with driver and English speaking guide to tour us around the temples. There are loads of them covering an area of around 400 square kilometres.

Temples are overgrown by the jungle

It was a relief, after tramping around a multitude of temples in the heat, to get on a boat and visit a village built on stilts on wetlands adjacent to a huge lake. Their way of life intrigued me. This was a miniature Venice in South East Asia, but with less ornate architecture – there is only so much you can do with bamboo and thatch, or corrugated iron! The houses are perched on stilts over the water, which at that time of year was high with the monsoon rains. Children went to and from school by boat, demonstrating from an early age their competence in boatmanship. Electricity comes from car batteries, charged at a nearby dry-land village. That allows them to watch TV and enjoy karaoke at night.

Water village

Around 3 million Cambodians were tortured and killed during the reign of terror under the dictator, Pol Pot, who led the Khmer Rouge totalitarian regime (1975–79) that imposed severe restrictions on the Cambodian people. Ethnic groups, intellectuals, lawyers, educators, army generals, and anyone with a connection with foreigners were rounded up and killed. They were buried in mass graves in what became known as the Killing Fields. Many of these graves were shallow, and tigers and wild dogs often dug up the bodies, scattering human bones over the area. These bones have been collected, and heaps of them are now on display in glass cases at the various Killing Fields, a macabre reminder of man's inhumanity to man.

Killing Fields Memorial

A new experience on this trip was to have a foot massage, by fish eating the dead skin cells off the feet and ankles. Sitting on the edge of an aquarium full of wee black fish, you plunge your feet into the water, and the fish attack you like piranhas. They only nibble away at the dead cells on the surface of the skin, but it is the most ticklish experience I have ever endured. I was in uncontrollable hysterics. For a few minutes, I became the leading tourist attraction in Siem Reap as hordes of passers-by stopped to gaze in wonder at my manic laughter. It was only when Ray and Philipp stopped laughing at me and put their feet in, that the fish diverted their attention to them, and the tickling eased as fewer fish ate me. It then became quite relaxing as they cleaned the feet and lower legs, leaving nice smooth skin. I was tempted to put my face in to see if they could improve on that.

The Cambodians impressed me by their friendliness, and their ability to speak English. They were always asking: "Which country are you from?"

"Scotland."

"Scotland, population 5 million people, capital city Edinburgh, is part of the United Kingdom along with England, Northern Ireland

and Wales." This happened time and time again with waitresses, and even the vendors at the souvenir stalls at the temples.

Ray also persuaded me to accompany him on a tour of Vietnam. Starting with a boat trip to Halong Bay, with its surreal pinnacles of limestone rising from the sea, we explored an enormous cavern inside one of the islands, and did a tour of Hanoi. The food in Vietnam was superb, a blend of Oriental and French cuisines, with many small courses and regional variations.

The people were welcoming everywhere, and it was hard to believe that there had been what seemed to be an interminable war raging there, with the communist Viet Cong battling for independence through the 1950s under French colonialism, and against the Americans until they withdrew from Saigon (re-named Ho Chi Minh City) in 1975. Many atrocities were committed by both sides, but it was remarkable how resourceful the Viet Cong were in improvising weapons, creating hideous booby traps, digging miles of tunnels, and steadfastly refusing to accept subjugation by the military might of the French, and then the USA and Australia, in what was a prolonged and horrific war. Their guerrilla tactics proved effective, and the powerful modern armies with their aircraft, bombs, and tanks had to give up.

The tragedy is that when you see how well the Vietnamese seem to be doing now, and how welcoming they are, you have to ask: Why was that war necessary? So many lives were lost because of fear of an ideology. Communism spread throughout Vietnam, but not beyond it. It appears to be a prosperous and welcoming nation, with few similarities to the Russian-driven repressive communism that swept through Eastern Europe after World War II. As a visitor, you only gain a superficial glimpse of life, and general impressions may not always be accurate, but there was none of the austerity or restrictions that typified the European countries that endured communist rule for so long. Modern Vietnam presented itself as an open, welcoming, and prosperous country.

As when diving on ships that had been sunk in wartime, Vietnam and its memorials reveal the futility of war, and the death and destruction it causes.

Chapter 34

FELLOWSHIP

S itting near the front of the ferry at Batangas Pier, I fumed. It was already 15 minutes behind the scheduled sailing time, and seemed to be in no hurry to cast off. The crew stood around and waited. I waited. I had no option. It was their boat. And this was the Philippines, where nothing ever seems to leave on time. A young man came running along the quay and made his way down the gangplank on to the boat. He sat opposite me and wiped the perspiration from his forehead. The crew hauled the gangplank aboard and cast off.

I looked at the young man. Something familiar about that face. He looked at me. Was that a flicker of recognition? We glanced at each other on and off for a few minutes. His finger came up, his face brightened, and he exclaimed, "It's John!" It was Conor McEntee, a young Irishman from Belfast, with whom I had dived in 2007 at Gili Trawangan in Indonesia.

"What brings you here?" I asked.

"You!" he replied. "It was your stories of diving in the Philippines that inspired me to come to this part of the world. I am following the advice you gave me back then in Indonesia. I was diving at Coron last week, it will be Puerto Galera this week, and Panglao the week after that, all places you recommended. Your advice was spot on. I love the Philippines. I am sorry I only booked for three weeks. I should have made it three months."

He was the second person I had met at Gili Trawangan who had stepped off the ferry at Puerto Galera. On my previous visit, it was an English girl who had acted on my advice. Often, even in the most remote locations, I hear my name being called out. It comes from being a member of that informal worldwide fellowship of scuba divers.

I was heading this way to meet a Filipino friend, Rolly Baron, whom I had met on my ill-fated live-aboard trip diving the Coron wrecks. Making a series of diving programmes for TV, he had filmed me diving on the wrecks, interviewed me, and used some of my photos on his shows. Rolly was keen to encourage people into diving. My enthusiasm and knowledge of many of the world's best dive spots he had found inspirational, and was amazed that I had only started diving ten days before my sixty-first birthday.

We had promised to meet and dive together again, and he had phoned me to say that he was filming a conference of the Professional Scuba Divers Association at Puerto Galera. He wanted me to join him after it was over to cross to Anilao, where he rented an apartment, and we could dive together there.

Puerto Galera, the port of galleons, named when the Philippines was a Spanish colony, is a small town on a peninsula at the north end of Mindoro, a large, mountainous island. It is about five hours travelling time by bus and ferry from Manila – if everything runs on time. A sizeable population of Europeans, Americans, and Australians have settled there, many with Filipina wives or partners. Its main attraction is diving, and the centre of the action is the village of Sabang Beach, tucked into a bay on its north coast.

The village is compact and you can walk from one end to the other in ten minutes. Buildings crowd down to the waterfront with little space between them. There is only one street into the village: the rest is a maze of narrow alleyways where you often have to stand sideways to let someone pass. It is a place that has never been blessed with the touch of a town planner, but this is the Philippines where planning seems to be alien to their culture. They tend to do things on impulse here. Despite the congestion and frequent power cuts, it has character, but it is not to everyone's liking. If you want everything pretty and tidy, this is not the place to be, but its renowned marine biodiversity attracts divers from all over the world. Accommodation is available to suit every budget, food to suit every nationality. And here, more than anywhere else, I have formed many sustained friendships.

My three regular American buddies, Mike Colibert and Tony Kirksey from Oklahoma, and the irrepressible Mr-Ray-From-The-USA Casavant from Connecticut, were first encountered here in 2008, when they embarked on the Stella Maris on her way to Tubbataha Reef, along with Mark Hawkins and Jason Shaw, both of whom I have also met again, Mark in the Solomon Islands, Jason at Palau. Mike, Tony, and Ray have all come to visit me in Scotland. A long weekend visit to Scotland has become an annual event for Philipp Baumgartner from Germany, another annual dive buddy since we met at Palau in 2008. It was here I first buddied with David Schaffland from Canada in December 2006. I was the catalyst that brought together this group of friends who have teamed up, in various combinations, for diving among the Similan Islands in Thailand; at Lembeh Strait, Bunaken, Bali, Gili Trawangan, and Ambon in Indonesia; in the Solomon Islands; at Sipadan, Borneo; and at Puerto Galera, Tubbataha Reef, Dumaguete, Anilao, Bohol, South Leyte, and Davao in the Philippines. Each year they asked me for my itinerary and then selected the places they would like to join me.

Another significant encounter while diving at Sabang, was to be paired for an afternoon dive with Paul Allen, an excellent underwater photographer. Underwater photography, like all wildlife photography, demands a lot of patience, often staying in the environment of a particular subject until the fish will accept the photographer's presence. The problem is that the other divers don't want to hang about waiting for photographers. They want to get on and cover ground. To them, a photographer is just a nuisance. Paul preferred to dive solo. He didn't like having other people around, hounding him on, or disturbing the fish, and he was not at all keen on having to buddy with me. He was quite blunt about it.

"I don't like people diving with me, crowding me, and running out of air, forcing me to come up early."

"Good. I feel the same. Keep out of my way and we'll get on fine." I replied. The other divers did a routine dive. I prowled around taking my pictures and left him to take his, but as buddies, we maintained visual contact. When I found a Harlequin Shrimp, often a prized subject for photographers, I invited to him to have a look. From then on he let me know when he found something of interest. We were now working as a team. I was delighted when he indicated that *he* was low on air and had to surface, while I still had enough air for several more minutes. I had earned his respect. A few days later, he invited me to join him for a shore dive, just the two of us walking in from the beach, with no other divers milling around. We spent a glorious 90 minutes underwater in the bay, never more than about 200 metres from the dive shop, but finding plenty to photograph.

He invited me to his apartment to dine with him. His wife, Rey-an, cooked dinner while we talked and watched a slide show of his work from different parts of the world. His photography exemplified the standards of achievement I wanted to aspire to. Studying his work and listening to him talk, I learned more about underwater photography from him than from any other source. Our respect for each other grew into a lasting bond of friendship, and he and Rey-an joined me for some sailing on my yacht on the west coast of Scotland the following summer. I was stunned when he died of pancreatic cancer a couple of years later.

On my first dive at Sabang Beach, the veteran dive instructor and guide, Bob Kieran, 'Daddy Bob' as he was known locally (also now deceased), paired me with David Schaffland. David worked as a respiratory therapist in Saudi Arabia then and took time off for diving three or four times per year. It was a fortuitous meeting. We have dived together ever since and developed such an uncanny understanding that we can almost read each other's minds. Either of us may articulate a thought the other was just about to voice. This understanding, and my complete trust in his competence should anything go wrong, created a feeling of security when diving together. He is an accomplished landscape photographer, and after supporting me as a buddy, always keeping a watch while I was taking photos and guiding me back to the group, he took up underwater photography too. The dive guides knew our competence, the extent of our experience and knowledge of the area, and let us do our own thing. That allowed them to concentrate on guiding the others who were usually less experienced.

Despite the gap of a generation – I am older than his parents, and he is younger than my younger son – the age difference proved irrelevant. Although we may have looked like father and son, at times he treated me more like his kid brother, with the pained look of the elder sibling longing for the day when I would grow up – but that won't be for a while yet!

When dining out, we often engage in a bit of banter with the waitresses. He likes to seek advantage by putting me in my chronological place, telling them that I am his Dad, a cheap, foul stroke to try to gain an edge in competition for their attention. It might be argued that he is handsome, despite the extended forehead – his hairline only starts in line with his ears – and his sharp wit and undoubted charm never fails to raise a laugh among the girls. As the waitresses chatted away to each other in Tagalog he chipped in, "Be careful what you are saying now! We both know quite a bit of Tagalog, and I know when you say *kalbo*, (meaning bald) you are talking about me." The girls giggled.

And I chipped in, "And I know when you say, *guapo*, (handsome) you are talking about *me*!"

His eyes rolled heavenwards. "I apologise for my Dad. Modesty has never been one of his endearing characteristics."

When you dive, you accept there is always the small risk of something going wrong underwater. That is when you depend on your dive buddy to help you out in a crisis. Diving is therefore an activity that encourages the establishment of an ethos of support. Having a good buddy whose dive style and competence is similar to your own is therefore desirable. Relationships established underwater have provided a basis for lasting friendships on land. I cherish the bonds I have formed with these friends, and many others with whom I have dived. In hazardous conditions, it is comforting to know you have someone you can trust supporting you.

Nudibranchs (sea slugs with naked gills), and other sea slugs and marine flatworms tend to be colourful (the butterflies of the ocean). There are more than three thousands species, with more being discovered every year, thanks to the proliferation of digital cameras. As well as being colourful subjects, they are slow moving, and that makes it a lot easier to get close-up shots of them. They are therefore popular subjects for photographers. I studied the literature on these interesting animals to learn more about their lifestyle, what they ate, and from that I learned where to find them. As my knowledge grew, I posted some pictures on the internet on identification sites.

That brought me into fellowship with those who shared an interest in these animals. I was a regular customer at John Henderson's photography shop in Sabang Beach which had some marvellous pictures of them on its walls that he had taken himself. That established a bond with him and his charming assistant Sherilyn, who took the photos of me required for my visa extensions each year. I had to pass the shop to go to the market each day, and it became a regular spot to stop for a chat if they did not have any customers. Sadly, he succumbed to cancer. Friends of my vintage are becoming rare.

Nudibranchs can be very colourful

Over 3000 known species

High colouring is a defence warning – I don't taste good.

Posting pictures on identification websites led to communication with other photographers. Online friendships developed, and some of them came to the Philippines to dive with me.

Terry Gosliner, senior curator of Invertebrate Zoology at the California Academy of Sciences, and joint author of many identification books, wrote and asked me to meet him at Sabang. He was leading an expedition to study the marine biodiversity of the Verde Passage and wanted to meet me to discuss a nudibranch he had seen in one of my pictures. He reckoned it may be a new species, and I helped him locate a specimen to take back for scientific study to determine what it might be. Soon afterwards, the Bombay Natural History Society wrote to me seeking permission to publish some of my photos in an identification book it was producing. I was thrilled to be contributing, in a very small way, to the knowledge of the tropical marine environment, and gathering friends to fill the gaps among those of my age group who were dying off.

In an ageist society it has been a privilege, in my twilight years, to enjoy a lifestyle more often assumed to be the prerogative of younger people. In most physical activities, performance declines with age. However, when diving there is no stress on the joints, as there is on land. Having neutralised buoyancy, you are weightless. You can raise your entire body weight, plus the weight of your air tank and the lead weights you have to add to get you down there, simply by breathing in. The extra air in your lungs increases your buoyancy, and allows you to rise over wrecks and rocks, corals and reefs, and little or no muscular effort is required. Relax, take it easy, and you can stay underwater longer. Technique and superior performance of the experienced and elderly diver earns the respect and admiration of those much younger – and at my age nearly everyone else is much younger!

I feel privileged that so many of the younger people I have met and dived with have come to visit me in Scotland. That is not only good for my morale, it also seems to be a good antidote to the ageing process.

After one of my annual health checks for diving, my doctor summed up: "Whatever you are doing, keep on doing it!"

And I did.

Chapter 35

A NEW CAREER

My travels around the world had led to invitations to deliver illustrated talks, bringing the Galapagos Islands, Antarctica, Easter Island, the Pacific Islands, and South East Asia to audiences and photographic clubs all over Scotland. I never advertised. My engagements all arose from word being passed from one group to another. As my interest in diving developed and started to define my itineraries, I felt compelled to take up underwater photography, to share the undersea world with my audiences.

Sabang Beach provided an excellent location to develop my interest. The Puerto Galera peninsula, on the south side of the Verde Passage, is renowned for its marine biodiversity. It has everything a diver could want: spectacular deep dives, strong currents that attract large numbers of fish, sheltered bays with beautiful corals and walls, sandy bottoms with a fascinating variety of peculiar 'critters.' Its nudibranchs and flatworms offer great subjects for photographers, and it was in this field that I decided to specialise.

Sabang Beach

As my collection of pictures grew, I felt there was a need for an identification book focussing on the sea slugs and flatworms to be found in the Puerto Galera area. I published a field guide which earned me a reputation there as 'The Nudibranch Man,' bringing me into contact with dive guides from the other dive shops and their customers.

The next step in my career progression came when Rick Kirkham, the owner of Frontier Divers at Sabang Beach, suggested I should take a professional qualification as a divemaster. He could then employ me to guide other divers, especially photographers. That would allow him to separate photographers from divers who just wanted to cruise and observe. I was more than happy about that: *he* would be paying *me* to dive, instead of *me* paying *him* as a customer.

The teacher in me emerged when sharing my knowledge with the people I guided. The ocean was my classroom, and my clients' pleasure in photographing marine animals they had never seen before was my reward. Some wrote touching testimonials: *'Thank you for your outstanding educational and friendly guiding this week from all of us. The knowledge you shared will pay multiple dividends!'*

Two other dive shops called on me when they were under pressure. With three shops employing me, I was never short of work and my earnings paid for my accommodation for the six months of each year I spent abroad. As a free-lance guide, I could take a couple of weeks off from time to time to dive in neighbouring countries, at the places described in this book. My lifestyle had settled into an annual routine: six months of Spring and Summer in Scotland, sailing, gardening, delivering talks. And like a migrating bird, I flew out of Scotland each October for six months diving in South East Asia, while the winter storms ravaged the highlands of Scotland.

Divers are taken to a variety of sites, most of which have a general appeal and are often scenically attractive. I always asked new customers what they were interested in seeing and planned dives accordingly. Some of the best sites for photographers may not be attractive to the general diver, but offer a habitat for the kind of weird animals they love to capture on camera.

An American photographer told me in more than twenty years of diving he had never seen a blue-ringed octopus, a mimic octopus, or a flamboyant cuttlefish, and would love to get a photograph of any of these. I took him to a sandy bottom late that afternoon when the sun was going down, a time when these animals are likely to emerge from the sand and hunt for food – and he photographed all three in that one dive! That was one very happy customer.

Word of mouth is the most effective advertising. A couple of Americans walked into Frontier Divers and told Rick, "We were told to come here to dive and ask for a guide called John."

He called me over and said, "I have two people here wanting to meet you." At the end of their stay they took me out for dinner at one of the best restaurants in the village.

On coming ashore at the end of a dive at Action Divers, another shop I worked for, the owner spoke to a Chinese girl I had been guiding. "How was your dive today?"

"Brilliant. John found so many things I have never seen before and I got loads of great photos. I want him as my guide for *every* dive from now on."

The owner looked at me. "Are you available for the next two weeks?"

Life was good. My customers' satisfaction thrilled me. I was diving three, sometimes four times daily if there was a night dive. I walked home after my day's work with a spring in my step. My body glowed with health and vigour.

But one day, a story I remember from my childhood came back to haunt me. It was entitled: Pride Comes Before A Fall.

Chapter 36

PARALYSED

The circular steel hatch clanged against the bulkhead and the locking wheel spun to ensure an air-tight seal. A voice crackled through the intercom: "Oxygen on. Pressurising to twenty metres." The nurse in the hyperbaric chamber with me handed me an oxygen mask. "Hold it tight on your face to prevent any air getting in."

Lying flat on my back with nothing to do, I became anaesthetised by the rhythmic hiss of my breathing. The mask fell from my face.

"Wake up, John!" The nurse placed it over my nose again. "Sorry, but you need to stay awake and hold it on.'

Fitted with sensors to monitor my oxygen intake, the mask was bulky and obscured my view. This made it impossible to read a book. Without any visual stimulus, I battled to stay awake. The only solution was to exercise my mind. I reflected on the day's events, before and after the attack of The Bends (Decompression Sickness, DCS).

On waking that morning, I thought a day off was overdue as I had been working without a break for three weeks. I walked down to the beach and into Frontier Divers to see what was happening. It was all bustle, with preparations for a large number of divers. The short-cropped fair head of Rick Kirkham was bent over a tank fitting a regulator. His eyes lit up when he saw me.

Verde Island – my last dive

"Ah, John! Anthony has just called in sick. We are short of a guide for a boatload of divers going to Verde Island. Can you help us out?" Well, it was Rick who'd persuaded me to take my professional qualification, enabling me to live there for six months of each year at minimal expense. I couldn't refuse.

"Aye, no problem." My rest day can wait, I thought, and set up my gear ready for loading on to the boat.

The common cause of decompression sickness is a rapid ascent from depth. In my case, however, it had been a slow, careful ascent accompanying an inexperienced diver breathing from my tank after he had run out of air. He had experienced no problems on completing the dive. Why had I suffered an attack?

It had been the first dive of the day, entering the water at about 9 a.m. and surfacing after only 30 minutes with my out-of-air diver, but DCS is a complex condition that may be caused by a variety of factors. The body does not dispose of nitrogen as effectively when under pressure at depth, as it does when breathing air at surface pressure. The doctor reckoned that diving without a break for over three weeks had led to a build-up of residual nitrogen in my blood stream. In the tropical climate of the Philippines, the drying effect of air-conditioning while asleep may have caused a degree of de-hydration, also a possible contributing factor. And maybe age had something to do with it. Although 75 years old at that time, I had been bouncing around like a 25 year-old. I may have grown old, but I hadn't grown up!

DCS can affect movement, touch, and life support systems such as breathing and heartbeat. Symptoms may include numbness or a paralysis of the lower body that may creep upwards, and victims may be paralysed for life from the neck down – or die. I knew of two casualties near me in Scotland; one wheelchair-bound for the rest of his life, the other dead.

On surfacing at the end of the dive, I'd felt a brief shock, like a rubber bullet hitting me. Later, I discovered I couldn't pee. I started breathing from the emergency oxygen cylinder we kept on board as a precautionary measure, skipped the second dive, and walked to the doctor after coming ashore in the early afternoon.

Dr Arroyo suspected decompression sickness, but first she inserted a catheter to drain the urine from my distended bladder which was causing considerable pain. She sent a sample to the lab to test for urinary infection, put me on a treatment bench with a drip to counter dehydration, and gave me oxygen, the standard first aid in dealing with DCS. Ninety minutes later the test results arrived – no infection.

"It has to be decompression sickness, John. We must get you to Batangas to the hyperbaric chamber for recompression."

By this time, Rick had appeared to see how I was. He said he would arrange a boat for the twenty-mile trip across the Verde Passage to Batangas, a major seaport city on the mainland.

"Go to your apartment for your insurance details and personal essentials for a stay in hospital. We'll meet you at the pier," said Dr Arroyo. I swung my legs off the treatment bench, staggered, and clutched at the bench for support.

"Hey, my legs feel like rubber!"

"That's paralysis setting in," said Dr Arroyo. "A nitrogen bubble compressing the spinal cord is the likely cause. We have no time to waste. I will call the hospital and tell them it is urgent that you get into the chamber and arrange an ambulance to meet you at the pier at Batangas. I will come with you with a drip and cylinder of oxygen. We must keep you hydrated and breathing oxygen."

My legs were difficult to control, becoming wayward and uncertain every time I took a step. She called a policeman who was standing outside. "May I ask you to help this gentleman to his apartment to collect some things for a stay in hospital and then bring him to the pier?"

That was embarrassing. Staggering home in the clutches of a policeman raised shocked looks from people I knew, and many I didn't, but there was no time to stop and explain. Aboard the boat, I lay on a bench. Dr Arroyo plumbed me into the drip and oxygen supply and monitored my blood pressure and heart rate during the twenty-mile voyage.

When we docked, the ambulance crew eased me off the bench, stretchered me into the ambulance, and strapped me in for a high-speed run to the hospital: blue light flashing, klaxon blaring, plumbed into an oxygen supply and a saline drip, checking blood pressure and heart rate – the whole VIP fanfare. A medical team awaited my arrival with a trolley and wheeled me into the hospital.

"Are you able to stand?"

"I don't know. They carried me off the boat."

Two nurses eased me off the trolley. My legs crumpled. They caught me and rolled me back on.

The next question was: "Who is paying for this? Do you have insurance? Or a credit card?"

I handed over my Divers Alert Network (DAN) Gold Standard Insurance card. "Good. We have worked with DAN before. They are very reliable, but we must telephone them first for permission to take action. I am sure there will be no problem, but we must get you into the chamber as soon as possible. In case we can't contact them immediately, are you willing to guarantee payment by credit card? Each session in the chamber will cost $4000?"

I didn't have much choice. It was essential to get treatment before the paralysis spread to my upper body as well. I showed them my credit card: "Okay, let's get on with it."

"We'll put you in the hyperbaric chamber for five hours, pressurise it, and you will breathe only oxygen. In the final hour we will decompress the chamber slowly to simulate the ascent from a dive." They laid me on a conveyor and rolled me through the circular hatch. A nurse crawled in after me and eased my body on to a bunk. He fed the conveyor back out and slammed the hatch shut.

I glanced around. Nothing much to see. The word 'coffin' entered my mind, and the questions: "Will I ever walk again? How will I react if I am immobilised for the rest of my life?"

"Hey, steady on, John!" I told myself. My training and the knowledge it gave me kicked in. With prompt treatment the probability of recovery is high, and although 10 hours had passed since I had surfaced and felt the first effects, I felt optimistic. I thought of my friend, Paul Johns, who had suffered a severe attack of DCS. Unconscious on surfacing, he had experienced total paralysis, thirteen sessions in a hyperbaric chamber and six months treatment. He was back on his feet and walking, albeit slowly. That gave me hope. But would I be able to dive again? That was a step too far. I had to get back on my feet first. To be truthful, I didn't feel death knocking on my door. This was just another setback in life's journey, and I felt sure I hadn't reached the terminus yet.

I imagined my late mother's reaction: "That Boy! He worries me sick! He just doesn't know when to stop!" She was right about that. Something within me always seemed reluctant to put on the brakes. I should have taken at least one day off each week to allow the nitrogen to de-gas out of my blood, but I had been so conceited and thought I was superman. And now I had learned a lesson the hard way. Aye, pride *had* come before a fall. I blasted myself for having no common sense.

I visualised my father, smiling at me: 'Och, you'll soon be back on your feet.' A steadfast influence when I was a boy, his reassurance was still empowering, even though he had died over thirty years before. The memories of my parents' contrasting reactions revived images of childhood.

People who have experienced near-death events, such as falling from a roof, or a tree, often report seeing their whole life flash before them. My life didn't flash past. With five hours to spend in the chamber it trundled past, and I saw a way of life that has gone: the clip-clop of horses' hooves on the street and the clatter of milk bottles delivered to doorsteps in the early morning; the sulphurous smell of smoke from coal fires lingering in the still, frosty air; the poor standard of housing in the 1940s; military preparations for D-Day; the grim conditions of employment. I reflected on the strictures of the education system, the freedom to play games on the street, my passion for football, and emergence as a young adult in the optimism of the 1950s when Rock 'n Roll was born and, according to Prime Minister Harold MacMillan at that time, "You've never had it so good."

"Aye, that's what I thought yesterday!" I mused.

The sense of adventure that had landed me here, I saw in embryonic form in the boy leaping from high sand dunes at the shore, diving into the dark, oily waters of the harbour, defying the commands of parents and teachers in exploration of forbidden places.

My time-travel back to Irvine, the small industrial town in the west of Scotland in which the foundations of my life had been laid, had solved the problem of staying awake. I began to enjoy lying motionless in the chamber, visualising a replay of events from my childhood.

I could write a book about this, I thought.

Chapter 37

FESTINA LENTE

"Pressure off. Oxygen off. Opening door." The metallic voice of the intercom disrupted the flow of memories.

"Okay John, take the mask off now," said the nurse in the chamber with me. He stowed it away. The hatch opened. The conveyor was rolled in and I was rolled out. Three nurses were waiting to assist me.

"Now, let's see if you can stand?"

Two nurses eased me on to the floor. My legs supported me this time, but the nurses held on to me as I swayed.

"That's fine. Now sit down. Keep your head still, but look at my finger and follow it by moving your eyes only." I managed that.

"Now hold my hands," said the girl standing in front of me.

"This is an unexpected treat." I grinned at her.

"Try to squeeze my hands. Good, plenty of strength there."

She kneeled down, hit my knees with a hammer, and found a reflex. Then she braced my right leg. "Try to push against me." She did the same for the left leg. "Now stand up, and let's see if you can take a step towards me."

The two other nurses supported me as I swayed, trying to maintain my balance. The signal from my brain to the leg muscles seemed slow, but with arms held out to the side for balance and two nurses beside me in case I fell, I leaned to my left to take the weight off my right foot. I managed to raise it and sling it forward. It landed with a flat-footed slap on the floor. I swayed, and the nurses caught me.

"I'm okay. Let me go."

I did the same with the other foot. Two steps. I swayed, but maintained my balance.

"Good. That's enough for now. We mustn't overdo it. We'll let you go to bed now." They eased me into a wheelchair.

"Well done, John," said the nurse as he wheeled me to my room. "That was an encouraging start."

"It's certainly an improvement on when I arrived."

"You did fine, but don't rush it. You need to give yourself time."

He eased me off the wheelchair, on to the bed, and tucked me in. I was about as helpless as a baby. It was now 2:30 a.m. I fell asleep immediately.

When I woke up, I noticed breakfast had been left on the table near the foot of the bed. I swung my legs over the side of the bed to walk to the table. I staggered. Clinging to the bed, I dragged myself along and dumped myself on the chair. The blood drained from my head. I thought I was going to pass out. Reaching for the bed, I hauled myself back on to it and lay there, gasping. The room began to spin, and I broke out in a sweat. A darkness seemed to envelop me. "Is this the end?" I wondered. At last the spinning stopped. The cold breakfast had lost its appeal, and I fell asleep again. I was more careful about getting out of bed after that. It didn't do much for my morale, but like the Scottish weather, that soon changed.

Later that morning, the doctor breezed in with the team of nurses from the hyperbaric chamber. He had the results of blood tests taken when I arrived at the hospital.

"Mr McMillan, I am so pleased to meet you. You must tell me your secret."

"What secret?"

"You are the most fit and healthy patient I have ever seen! (He would have changed his tune if he'd seen me clinging to the bed three hours earlier!) The people we get in here with decompression sickness are usually obese, diabetic, smoke, take too much alcohol, have high cholesterol, high blood pressure, heart problems, but your results are perfect. I can't believe you are 75 years old. And you are still diving. Look at you. You have the body of a 25 year-old!"

"Och, I know. That's what all the girls tell me," I muttered modestly.

The two nurses giggled and nodded.

"Calm down, girls!" He turned his attention back to me.

"But how do you do it? Most people here in the Philippines are dead at your age. Do you work out in the gym?"

"No. I just keep active, in body and mind. I played a lot of football when I was young, and since I retired I've travelled the world: trekking up mountains, through jungles, kayaking, sailing, diving, writing, giving talks back home in Scotland."

"It's good that you have so many interests. And with your general state of health, I think you should recover soon. We'll give you another session in the chamber after lunch."

That perked me up. Maybe I could dive again! But then I heard the quiet words of Hector MacKenzie, my Latin teacher at Irvine Royal Academy: *Festina Lente*. Make haste slowly. I had to keep a grip on reality.

I doubted that diving would feature in my life after my release from hospital, but a life without the thrill of exploration underwater was a depressing prospect. My view of the future was that of a man gazing at an infinite desert: arid, colourless, featureless. This was no good: I had to shake off the negativity.

I had often counselled divers against rushing around in an attempt to see more during a dive. "Go slow, look, and you may be surprised at what you find." There is plenty to see on a coral reef teeming with colourful marine life, but the muddy bottom of a bay may appear devoid of life. However, the diver who takes time to examine a sand or muddy bottom may find more than was apparent at first glance. Those two stones metamorphose into the eyes of a stargazer, a plump fish that buries its body in soft sand, it's upward facing mouth waiting to snap any passing small fish. A tiny puff of sand betrays the nervous twitch of the almost invisible, glass-like body of a transparent shrimp, with only minute flecks of colour at its joints. A round stone suddenly abandons its disguise and flashes a pattern of neon-like blue rings as the diver approaches, revealing its true identity as a blue-ringed octopus – tiny, cute, eagerly sought-after by photographers, but with a deadly poisonous bite.

Taking time to scrutinise the environment may reveal more than at first may be apparent, an appropriate reminder in my current situation. When contemplating my future, it would be wise to exercise patience and explore my options.

While reviewing the events that had shaped my early life, I had become aware that I had been engaged in a continuous process of adaptation: in how we lived, worked, played, and socialised. I had learned to adapt all through my life. Not all the changes had been welcomed, but happiness is a choice. Victimhood is also a choice. And I had the power to choose between them.

I was inspired by the example of the people who inhabit many of the countries of South East Asia. They live with considerable uncertainty. The land they occupy may change its nature, within moments, in an earthquake that could bring death on a large scale. They may fall victim to a resurgence of volcanic activity from a mountain that has lain dormant and benign for hundreds of years. They often fall victim to typhoons that may sweep them to their deaths in landslides or floods. Or they may look in horror when the sea that has been their livelihood, the provider of food for generations, turns malevolent as a dreaded tsunami thunders down on flimsy coastal villages, sweeping all before it: cars, buses, houses, and the people in them. They are no strangers to catastrophe. Many know grief and horror on a scale most of us can never imagine.

Although I have experienced many earth-shaking moments in that part of the world, most had only mild effects. When you see the refrigerator dancing across the floor in the middle of the night, it can have a disturbing effect in a mind befuddled by sleep. We become disoriented by events peculiar to what we perceive as normal. But to the people for whom these events may occur at any time, that *is* normality. Catastrophic events are shrugged off. Life goes on.

While writing several chapters of this book on the island of Mindoro in the Philippines, I have experienced earthquakes. My apartment has trembled, and sometimes I have too, wondering how big this one is going to be, but I have experienced no catastrophic damage – yet. A bit further south on Negros, many people lost their lives when an earthquake measuring 6.9 on the Richter scale struck. A few weeks prior to that, many lives were lost in dramatic floods and landslides when more than a month's rainfall fell in two hours. I had been diving there a week before the floods, and a week after the earthquake. I had been lucky. Many of the local people had not. Those who survived got on with life. And I was determined to do the same.

The night before before she died, my wife counselled me: "Live every day to the full. There is nothing to fear, except fear itself."

Her words still guide me.

Chapter 38

ON THE MEND

After my second session in the hyperbaric chamber, the nurses took me through the same exercises as before, then added some.

"I want you to stand with your feet together, and stretch your arms out horizontally."

My arms swayed up and down, like the wings of an aircraft landing in a strong sidewind, as I tried to maintain my balance.

"Not bad. Now I want you to do the same, but close your eyes this time."

With no visual terms of reference, I toppled to one side but the two other nurses grabbed me, arresting my fall.

"Okay, you're not ready for that yet. Let's see if you can walk. Just try two steps." I managed that; cumbersome, but I did it.

"Good. Now let's see if you can walk a bit further. Come towards me." She stood back a pace and moved back again as I approached. I managed four shaky steps with arms held out for balance and legs flinging forward, like a puppet on a string – but I was walking!

"Well done, that's enough,' said the nurse in charge. 'How do you feel?"

"I feel like taking a walk."

"Good, but let's not rush it. This time I want you to try to walk along this white line on the floor by placing the heel of one foot against the toe of the other." She demonstrated.

I tried it. Useless! No coordination. I was like a drunk. I couldn't place heel against toe without falling. The nurses caught me.

"Ach! Let me try again." My second attempt was no better. The nurse read the disappointment on my face.

"Don't worry. It will come. You are making good progress. Don't forget you couldn't even stand when you arrived here. We'll give you a rest day tomorrow, and have you back for another session in the chamber the day after."

That gave me time to practice. I was determined to master these exercises. The slight progress I had made gave me the confidence to send a text to my two sons: *In hospital having a recovery from The Bends. Was paralysed from the waist down, but after two sessions in a hyperbaric chamber I am on my feet, learning to walk again. More sessions in the chamber to follow.*

Donald, my older son, replied as expected: *Glad to hear you are recovering. Let us know if you need any help.*

Euan, my younger son and a professional diver, also replied as expected. *Glad to hear you are on the mend. I can get a flight tomorrow. Where exactly are you?*

NO! There is no need. I'll soon be mobile again. I replied. I knew he would give me hell for getting into trouble. He had a bit of my mother in him.

OK, but keep us informed. And if you are tempted to dive again, DON'T! Aye, that was my mother speaking, right enough!

Spoilsport! I replied.

Why not spend some time writing about your thoughts in the chamber?

That suggestion held more appeal. The memories of childhood while I was in the chamber gave me something to work on, a story to weave into the family history I had been writing, on and off, for several years. I had been writing articles for a local heritage website, so I already had a readership.

The thought of no more diving was hard to bear, but I had to contemplate a different future. I could still share my knowledge and enthusiasm when invited to do talks. And I could write about my travels. Even if no one read what I wrote, it would allow me to re-live the memories of places, of diving, of the friends who had enhanced my life. Perhaps some of my descendants might read it and be inspired to seek what the world has to offer.

Recovery was still uncertain, but I was determined to face the challenge. The door of my hospital room was my way back to the world I loved to explore. I was determined to walk through it – and grasp whatever opportunities it offered.

I had stretched the boundaries of prudence too often in the past. The journey back to normality had to be taken in small steps, but I now had a route map to recovery. I was applying a bit of common sense at last.

After two further sessions in the chamber and practicing the exercises in my room, I was on my feet again. The doctor felt I could be released from hospital, but only after I had the consent of the urologist. I couldn't pee after my last dive, and the doctor had inserted a catheter. They had taken it out a couple of times in the hospital to try to stimulate my bladder to perform as normal, but without success. When inserting the new catheter, the nurse had rammed it against the bladder wall. A blood clot had formed and blocked the catheter, and within a few hours I was in agony again. It had to be withdrawn and a new one inserted, with more care. The urologist had been called in, and an ultra-sound scan revealed an enlarged prostate. Damage to the nervous system in the lower abdomen, caused by the attack of The Bends, was also a possible contributing factor to my inability to urinate. He prescribed medication.

The insurers were keen to get me home, as medical care in the UK would be free under our National Health Service. The hospital bill had already come to around £30,000, and they still had to meet the cost of flying me back home. But the thought of a catheter blockage during a long-haul flight of 14 hours was not appealing.

I was relieved when the urologist insisted that I must be accompanied by a nurse experienced in dealing with such matters. I was even happier when the insurers agreed, upgraded my flight to Business Class, and told me a nurse would meet me at Manila Airport in the Business Class Lounge to accompany me home. Travelling Business Class with a pretty Filipina nurse to hold my hand and chat to me all the way back to Scotland? Life wasn't so bad after all.

A friend escorted me to the airport, and I sat in the KLM Business Class Lounge, waiting for my attractive Filipina nurse to greet me. A middle-aged, balding man approached.

"Mr John McMillan? I am Mario, your nurse, to escort you home." My fantasy dissolved. The insurers had flown Mario out from Rome, Business Class, put him up in a hotel in Manila, and flew us both back to Inverness, Business Class, where my son, Euan, took over at the airport. Mario then flew back to Rome the following day. That must have added another £10,000 to the bill.

Although not quite the nurse I had hoped for, Mario took good care of me, and I could not have asked for better treatment from the KLM staff on the aircraft, and the ground staff at Manila and Amsterdam. I had a wheelchair to meet me, priority on and off the aircraft and through immigration, and transport to my connecting flight to Inverness. It was the best long haul flight I'd ever undertaken.

My doctor in Lochcarron had been briefed, and saw me the morning after I arrived home. I made good progress, walking daily, increasing distance and pace, but further attempts to stimulate the bladder by hauling out the catheter not only failed, but twice resulted in urinary infections. The doctor warned me that an operation might be required to fit a permanent catheter, connected to the bladder by a stoma through the wall of my abdomen. Maybe that message got through to the bladder. After seven weeks without a pee, the plumbing started working again.

I asked the doctor if I could dive again. The answer was an emphatic, "No!" He wagged a finger at me: "You are lucky to be alive. Statistics suggest that people who've had a DCS Type II are more likely to have a further attack. The next one could could be fatal, or you could be paralysed from the neck down. For someone with your active lifestyle that might seem worse. You can swim, but no diving."

"What about travel?"

"That should be no problem – as long as you behave yourself."

"What? And change the habits of a lifetime?"

"Well, at least as far as diving is concerned. The question is: how will you fill the void now that you can't dive?"

"After breaking my Achilles Tendon in Fiji, I was immobilised with my leg in plaster for three months, but I turned it to advantage by starting to write about my travels. I contribute articles to a local heritage website, and have ideas in mind for two or three books. I could do worse than escape the Scottish winter and sit on a tropical island writing. I could write during the day, with exercise breaks for walking and swimming, and socialise with my diving friends in the evenings."

"That sounds like a plan," he said. "And what about when you are at home?"

"As well as writing, I have been delivering talks for several years, based on my travels and books. I have two bookings for talks in Aberdeen, as well as for the South-West Ross Field Club, the Scottish Wildlife Trust, and The Howard Doris Centre. And I have some ideas for altering my garden to make it easier to manage when I get old."

He looked at my date of birth and smiled. "I don't see too much evidence of that yet!"

The following winter I was back in the Philippines again, but diving was not on the agenda. I enjoyed sitting on my balcony writing, and the research proved stimulating and kept my mind active. My body still demanded exercise, but of a less intense kind: walking and swimming.

Two years on, I began to experience sudden chest pains – Angina. A scan revealed narrowing of the main artery to the heart in five places, but not critically, and a course of medication was recommended to control it. Maybe I was getting old after all.

That put a different perspective on my attack of The Bends. I now look upon it as a fortuitous occurrence. If it hadn't happened, and I had continued diving for another two years, an Angina attack deep underwater could have had a serious outcome. In any case, having been diagnosed with Angina, I would have had to give up diving.

Travel presents challenges. You must adapt to circumstances beyond your control, something every traveller needs to keep in mind. Whether storms, cancelled flights, no room at the hotel that you booked months ago, accident or injury, travel teaches you to adapt. Those who remain positive, cheerful, creative, supportive, and respectful of others can make life enjoyable for themselves, and for those with whom they interact.

By adapting to the loss of my wife to cancer, and my changing circumstances on retirement, I have enjoyed a life of adventure, excitement, education, exploration. I still experience the joy of learning and feel I am still growing – and maybe one day I might even grow up!

It has been said to me many times, "You are so lucky to have such a lifestyle." But it is not a matter of luck. We are free to set our own course in life. We make choices. Some may not be good, but we can learn from them and adapt. We have the power to alter course. When circumstances beyond our control enforce change, we must adapt. Having adapted to the loss of my wife, my travelling lifestyle has kept the ageing wheels in motion, developed a new career, and brought me a host of new friends. And, now in my eighties, I continue to enjoy life at home, and travelling to far-off places.

I am just not as *vigorous* as I used to be.

Maybe I'm learning a bit of common sense at last – but I wouldn't bet on it!

THE END